My Mother and I

ALSO BY INGRID SEWARD

By Royal Invitation
Royalty Revealed
Diana: An Intimate Portrait
Sarah, Duchess of York
Royal Children of the 20th Century
Prince Edward
The Last Great Edwardian Lady
The Queen and Di
William and Harry
William and Harry: The People's Princes
Diana: The Last Word
The Queen's Speech
My Husband and I
Prince Philip Revealed

My Mother and I

The inside story of the King and our late Queen

INGRID SEWARD

**SIMON &
SCHUSTER**

London · New York · Sydney · Toronto · New Delhi

First published in Great Britain by Simon & Schuster UK Ltd, 2024

Copyright © Ingrid Seward, 2024

The right of Ingrid Seward to be identified as the author
of this work has been asserted in accordance with
the Copyright, Designs and Patents Act, 1988.

3 5 7 9 10 8 6 4

Simon & Schuster UK Ltd
1st Floor
222 Gray's Inn Road
London WC1X 8HB

Simon & Schuster: Celebrating 100 Years of Publishing in 2024

www.simonandschuster.co.uk
www.simonandschuster.com.au
www.simonandschuster.co.in

Simon & Schuster Australia, Sydney
Simon & Schuster India, New Delhi

The author and publishers have made all reasonable
efforts to contact copyright-holders for permission, and
apologise for any omissions or errors in the form of credits
given. Corrections may be made to future printings.

A CIP catalogue record for this book is
available from the British Library

Hardback ISBN: 978-1-3985-1517-8
eBook ISBN: 978-1-3985-1519-2

Typeset in Palatino LT Std by Palimpsest Book Production Ltd,
Falkirk, Stirlingshire

Printed and Bound in the UK using 100% Renewable
Electricity at CPI Group (UK) Ltd

MIX
Paper | Supporting
responsible forestry
FSC
www.fsc.org   FSC® C171272

'There is an enduring tenderness in the love of a mother
to a son that transcends all other affections of the heart'
– Washington Irving

CONTENTS

INTRODUCTION

King Charles III, despite his old-fashioned sympathies, is a twenty-first-century gentleman at heart; an ageless and quintessentially British character trying to do his best in a world whose modern innovations have perplexed many of his contemporaries.

An idealist with an inborn sense of kindness, he has always believed in others and wanted to help them. He feels passionately about the quality of life for our descendants and the future of our planet. For the last fifty years, he has been speaking out about all number of issues that are top of the political agenda today, from climate change, pollution and deforestation to simpler things like the value of recycling and rewilding.

He was a shy child and still suffers when meeting large numbers of people, but he is courteous. He never passes a footman in a palace corridor or a stranger while walking in the countryside without acknowledgement, whatever his mood. While others of a lesser social standing might ignore the staff – he loathes the word 'servants' – he is meticulous about saying thank you.

Charles is more like his mother than he would admit. The late Queen was painfully shy, and never comfortable with strangers, but she was very gentle and always listened to what they had to say. When she'd had enough, she would say 'Reaaaally' as a signal to her ladies-in-waiting to move her on. The controversial and renowned children's author Roald Dahl once told me he was seated next to the Queen at a luncheon at Buckingham Palace. Although Dahl was prone to a little exaggeration, he assured me that the Queen was one of the dullest people he had ever met. An arrogant genius, Dahl was never going to make it easy for her – and neither was the Queen in return. She insisted on talking about horses and, as he had no interest in horses whatsoever, he failed to respond with any kind of animation and the conversation lapsed. Unembarrassed, the Queen merely turned to the person on her other side.

'The Queen trained feelings out of herself in order to avoid any confrontation,' former Conservative statesman Douglas Hurd observed. The Queen's former press secretary, the late, enigmatic Martin Charteris, who started working for her when she was Princess Elizabeth, agreed. 'The Queen is not good at showing affection. She'd always be doing her duty.' Charteris worked at Buckingham Palace for over twenty years and claimed the Queen really had very little to do with Charles. 'He'd have an hour after tea with Mummy when she was in the country, but somehow even those contacts were lacking in warmth. His father would be rather grumpy, about almost anything. And neither of them was there very much.'

It was a terribly old-fashioned, upper-class upbringing. The royal family never spoke about their difficulties, and if any of them had a problem they never talked it over. They only spoke about the most trivial of things and, as a result, awkward issues were left in abeyance until it was too late. The late Diana, Princess of Wales, was the only exception to this. She would wait in the page's vestibule next to the Queen's sitting room and as soon as any visitor had departed, she would push her way in and throw herself on the Queen's mercy, frequently sobbing and telling her mother-in-law how much Charles hated her. Not surprisingly, the Queen had no idea what to do. Emotional confrontation of this sort was totally alien to someone whose upbringing insisted that manners were more important than feelings. As a result, she did nothing. It was a low point in her relationship with her son and, as the marriage spiralled out of control, Charles was reduced to shouting down the telephone at his mother to try to make her understand.

In his 1994 biography of the Prince, Jonathan Dimbleby paints an unhappy picture of Charles and his mother, saying the Prince bitterly recalled a childhood during which the nursery staff, not his 'emotionally reserved' parents, were the people 'who taught him to play, witnessed his first steps, punished and rewarded him, helped him put his first thoughts into words'.

Over the years, Charles and his mother mended their

relationship and it became one of mutual respect. Like many of us, once Charles has time to reflect on his relationships, he sees things in a different way.

'They mind about each other, even if they don't show it,' the Queen's cousin, the late Margaret Rhodes, confirmed. 'The Queen loves Charles deeply. It's just that they have a different outlook and sometimes they don't agree.'

When I talked to Prince Charles about his old school, Gordonstoun, some years ago over tea at Highgrove, I said I imagined it was brutal. He was quick to defend his alma mater. 'It wasn't brutal,' he said. 'Just basic. It certainly gave me a great deal of independence and taught me a lot in that area, which is what Eton did for William.'

The Queen never understood Charles's pampered lifestyle and found it rather mystifying, as by nature Charles is not a selfish man, but a life of being deferred to often stopped him considering others. He has no sympathy for trivial ailments and combats his own sinus problems by sleeping in an oxygen tent. Tiredness or oversleeping are not acceptable excuses for missing even an hour's work, and he will never have a lie-in on a Sunday morning, even if he is feeling unwell. He is insistent on things being done correctly, and when his childhood teddy bear – who, according to Prince Harry, goes everywhere with his 'pa' – needs repairing and patching, he sends the teddy to his wife's couturier to be mended, with instructions to do it quickly so he can have him back.

Charles may be eccentric about his teddy bear, but he can be a wonderful entertainer when the occasion arises.

Before his marriage to Diana, Charles was at a dinner party given by business tycoon Nigel Broackes, who was known for his lavish entertaining. The Prince found himself sitting opposite the then rock star Gary Glitter and, according to Glitter, asked him: 'Gary, what are the main attributes to being a pop star?' Glitter was unable to answer as his mouth was full of baked Alaska. But the pair got along so well, they ended up on top of the grand piano in Broackes's elegant sitting room, singing 'Ying Tong Song', a nonsense song written by Prince Charles's friend Spike Milligan and frequently performed by The Goons.

The Queen was far wiser about her son than he ever gave her credit for, and she was acutely aware of his strengths and weaknesses. She privately acknowledged long before anyone else that his marriage to Camilla was inevitable and they would have to stop playing what she called 'this cat-and-mouse game' and get on with it. She knew it would be the making of him as a man and eventually as King. They both understood he was public property, but Charles bitterly resented the intrusion into his private life – less so now he is King, an indisputably public role.

As King, he still finds solace in solitary pursuits such as reading and music, and while he sits at his desk working into the small hours, music blares inside the room. It is always something dramatic and sometimes also sad – a little like his own life. His 'darling mama' is no longer here, and he realises she is a very hard act to follow. He has to do the job in his own style. His ideas for reshaping the monarchy are quite the opposite of what many feared would be a grandiose vision of its future. His vulnerability, his humour and his ability to reach out to his people as King is working. In the end, Charles earned the love and support that he craved all his life. He will not let her down.

1

LIKE MOTHER, LIKE SON

'Little Prince, now born into this world of strife and storm'
– Winston Churchill, 1948

Hereditary monarchy has, with a few exceptions, enabled us to become familiar with the future monarch from the moment of their birth. The modern tradition of royal parents and infants being photographed on the hospital steps may have replaced the more formal, stylised portraits taken by the fashionable photographers of the age, but the royal children's subsequent lives continue to be documented by a series of carefully lit, posed pictures. The heir's eventual role as Sovereign, with all its inherent responsibilities, has been familiar to them and us since their childhood, though their subjects give their allegiance not to just the individual, but to the whole family, who hand over the torch from generation to generation – a notion that may seem old-fashioned but provides a continuity that is indispensable to us in these challenging times.

Despite there being only twenty-two years between their births, Queen Elizabeth and King Charles had very different experiences growing up.

In April 1926, when Elizabeth was born, London was experiencing some of the greatest social and economic changes since the end of the First World War. The great Mayfair houses, with their staff of footmen, maids, housekeepers, cooks, valets and nursemaids, to name but a few, had been left empty during the war years, their occupants scattered around Europe, many never to return. For those that did, a life in domestic service was not as attractive as it once was; the world was opening up slowly but surely to a more emancipated outlook on class and working opportunities.

In the ivory tower of royalty, however, things were still much the same as they had always been and, like the upper classes, social lives revolved around the countryside sporting calendar. The royal houses in the capital stood empty during the shooting and hunting seasons, the furniture covered with dust sheets, only to be brought to life again during the London season.

The house where Princess Elizabeth was born was the London home of her maternal grandparents, the Earl and Countess of Strathmore, who also owned a Scottish estate and a country house in St Paul's Walden, Hertfordshire. The pillared, double-fronted Mayfair house at 17 Bruton Street no longer exists, but opposite at number 10 the 1930s facade of the royal couturier Norman Hartnell's showrooms bears testimony to the grandeur of the area. London was still the largest city in the world, with a population of almost 8 million people; the most popular newspapers of the day were the *Daily Mail* and the *Daily Express*, with over 1.5 million readers each.

An upstairs bedroom of the Strathmores' Bruton Street house, where the Duke and Duchess of York were living at the time, was converted into an operating theatre for the birth of the Duchess's child. The specialists in attendance on that rainy April night were Sir Henry Simpson and Walter Jagger. Simpson was known as much for his charm as for his skills as a highly respected obstetric surgeon. He had a large private practice with patients including Princess Mary and had been in attendance at the birth of both of her sons.

In the early hours of the morning of 21 April, Sir Henry decided to perform a Caesarean section on the 26-year-old Duchess of York because the baby was in the breech position. As was the custom, the Home Secretary, Sir William Joynson-Hicks, was present and sent a message to the Lord Mayor of London to advise him of the imminent birth. Nothing was mentioned about the Caesarean. If anything was ever said, it was described as a 'certain procedure'.

'I must have been one of the first people outside members of the family to see the princess,' recalls Mabell, Countess of Airlie, in her memoir. 'I called at 17 Bruton Street on 22 April, the day after her birth: although I little thought then I was paying homage to the future Queen of England, for in those days there was every expectation that the Prince of Wales (who was holidaying in Biarritz) would marry within the next year or two.'

9

At the time of her birth, the little Princess was third in line to the throne, immediately after her father and his glamorous elder brother, the Prince of Wales. Behind her were her uncles Prince Henry, who was later the Duke of Gloucester, and Prince George, later the Duke of Kent, as well as her aunt Mary, who became the Princess Royal.

The christening took place on 29 May in the private chapel at Buckingham Palace (which was later destroyed by a bomb). It was presided over by the Archbishop of York, Cosmo Gordon Lang, and there were multiple godparents: Lady Elphinstone (her aunt); Arthur, Duke of Connaught (great-great-uncle); Queen Mary and King George V (paternal grandparents); the Earl of Strathmore (maternal grandfather); and Princess Mary, Viscountess Lascelles (aunt). The baby was named Elizabeth Alexandra Mary – after her mother, her great-grandmother and her grandmother, respectively. She was baptised by water from the River Jordan, which had been sent from the Holy Land for the christening. The occasion was recalled by Mabell Airlie, who was in attendance to Queen Mary as one of her 'Ladies of the Bedchamber' that day: 'She was a lovely baby although she cried so much all through the ceremony that immediately after it her old-fashioned nurse [Clara Knight] dosed her well from a bottle of dill water – to the surprise of the modern young mothers present and to the amusement of her uncle, the Prince of Wales.'

Like most small children, the Princess was fond of animals, and when she was tiny played with her grandmother Lady Strathmore's two chows, whom she loved to stroke, and would clap and chuckle, beating her heels on the floor, when she saw them. Her other greatest delight was to pat her father's large hunters and see him ride away in his hunting kit from Naseby Hall in Northamptonshire. The Duke and Duchess took this house for the hunting season and the Princess spent much of the winter there, with her nanny, Clara Knight, in attendance. She also loved her grandfather King George V's grey parrot Charlotte and used to select lumps of sugar to give to the bird. Later, when the Duke and Duchess moved from the Strathmore residence in Bruton Street to their own home, at 145 Piccadilly, the soot-covered nursery windows were a great fascination for the little Princess. Not only could she see the working horses pulling their heavy carts outside, but when she heard the clop of multiple hooves, she knew she would catch sight of the soldiers and horses threading their way under the arch that led to Constitution Hill.

In the 1920s and for much of the 1930s, the idea that Princess Elizabeth might become Queen was hardly considered, least of all by the Yorks, who were simply looking forward to gradually expanding their family. They expected to be pushed down the line of succession by the children from any union the Prince of Wales might make, little realising what was to come.

Twenty-two years later, Prince Charles was born into completely different circumstances to those of his mother. From the moment of his birth, it was clear he was going to be King one day and he was treated accordingly.

In 1948, the United Kingdom was still coming to terms

with the end of the Second World War, a bitter conflict that ravaged so many towns and cities throughout the United Kingdom. London was a dirty, dark, gloomy place and even the grandest houses lacked central heating. Ice froze on the inside of windows in the winter and ineffective coal fires burned in the grates of the rooms that were in use. Dense fogs known as 'pea-soupers' were common, especially in central London. The fogs clung to the windows, leaving sooty deposits behind, and visibility was reduced to a few yards, making driving difficult or impossible. Coal arrived in horse-drawn carts, or on an open lorry, with the coal tipped from blackened sacks into the house's coal hole outside in the pavement. If the coalman was not on a specific delivery, he would drive around the quiet streets shouting out 'Coal!'

At Buckingham Palace, things were grander but equally unglamorous. The winter of 1947 had been exceptionally hard and coal had been rationed, and in Buckingham Palace's 300 or so rooms the only heat came from its equal number of open fires. The palace had its own coal porters, whose job it was to fill the coal scuttles, wheel them to the lift and trundle them along the corridors on a wooden trolley that could carry ten of them at a time. The palace had been bombed several times during the war and there was a large amount of renovation work being done. The state rooms were among the first to be refurbished, and the artwork, which had been stored for safekeeping in the cellars of Windsor Castle, had been rehung as to the specifications in the original notes made before the war as to exactly where they should go. Although many rooms were restored to their former glory, food was still being rationed, though the royal household had the advantage of being almost fully self-sufficient, with meats, game, dairy produce and certain fruit being provided by the royal estates.

The London Olympics had been held during the summer of 1948 amid the strictures of post-war austerity. The King had opened the games on 29 July and although Germany, Japan and Russia were absent, the events were just as powerful. Rowing was held at Henley in Oxfordshire, shooting at Bisley in Surrey and yachting at Cowes in the Isle of Wight. The main stadium at Wembley had a new cinder track and the Empire Pool nearby provided the focus for the water sports.

After marrying Philip Mountbatten in November 1947, the Princess was keen to have a baby as soon as she could. But even she had been surprised at how quickly she had become pregnant.

The excited crowd outside the railings of Buckingham Palace had been monitoring the comings and goings after Sir William Gilliatt, Princess Elizabeth's gynaecologist, had spent the previous night at the palace. Gilliatt had served as gynaecologist to the royal family for more than twenty years. After attending Princess Marina the Duchess of Kent at the births of Edward, Alexandra and Michael, he attended Princess Elizabeth at the birth of Prince Charles and later Princess Anne, at Clarence House. For the birth of Charles, he was assisted by an eminent medical team: Sir John Weir, the King's homeopathic physician; Sir John Peel, a Fellow of the Royal College of Obstetricians and Gynaecologists, who later became the Queen's surgeon gynaecologist; Mr Hall, the anaesthetist, from King's College Hospital; and the loyal midwife Sister Helen Rowe, who was present for the delivery of all four of the Queen's children.

The birth, at 9.14 p.m. on the foggy night of 14 November 1948, was not an easy one. The official bulletin, pinned to the palace gates, announced that 'Her Royal Highness and her son are doing well.' The doctors later revealed that Charles was born by Caesarean section, but such was the prudery of the age that this was never officially disclosed; even the Princess's friends were not informed. Breastfeeding was not spoken of and even pregnancy, especially a royal pregnancy, was a condition that polite society feigned to ignore.

In another indication of contemporary attitudes, Philip did not attend his wife during her confinement. Nor did a Minister of the Crown; ahead of the birth, King George VI had issued an official announcement stating he felt it was an 'archaic custom' and 'no longer a constitutional necessity'. When her labour started, remembered the couple's equerry Mike Parker, the royal family gathered in Parker's room to await news of the birth. The King was stretched out by the fire and the Prince was pacing the floor. Eventually Parker took him off for a game of squash. 'Well, time stretched a bit and he was getting restless,' Parker recalled. When the King's private secretary Tommy Lascelles brought the good news, Philip bounded upstairs into the Buhl Room, which had been converted into an operating

14

theatre. He then held his firstborn, still wearing his sporting flannels and open-necked shirt.

His wife remained unconscious from the general anaesthetic, but as soon as she woke up, Philip presented her with a bouquet of red roses and carnations, thoughtfully provided for the occasion by Parker. Elizabeth would later say that her husband's face was the last she saw before she slipped under the anaesthetic and the first she saw when she came around again.

Prince Philip's mother, Alice, had recently moved to the island of Tinos in Greece, to a house without a telephone, so he was obliged to send her a telegram with the news. She was thrilled and wrote to him at once: 'I think of you so much with a sweet baby of your own, of your joy and the interest you will take in all his little doings. How fascinating nature is, but how one has to pay for it in the anxious trying hours of the confinement.'

Elizabeth breastfed her young son and Charles spent the first month of his life in a round wicker basket in the dressing room adjoining his mother's bedroom. She then contracted measles and the doctors advised that she and the baby stay apart – there was no measles vaccine in those days and the disease is highly contagious. Charles was taken away from his mother, who went to Sandringham to recuperate, and put into the care of two Scottish-born nannies: Helen Lightbody and the nursery maid, Mabel Anderson. Mrs Lightbody, the senior of the two, had brought up Charles's uncle the Duke of Gloucester's children and was known to the Princess, while Mabel Anderson, still in her early twenties, had only recently put an advertisement in the 'Situations wanted' columns of a nursing magazine. When she was asked to go to Buckingham Palace for her interview and sat down with the Princess Elizabeth, she was amazed, but accepted the job. Mabel was a great favourite and quite a character, and she stayed on to look after all the Queen's children before leaving to work for Princess Anne at her country home, Gatcombe Park. But life there wasn't for her and Mabel soon chose to retire. Now in her late nineties, she is still very much part of the family, living out her days in a cottage on the Windsor royal estate.

Like all expectant mothers, the Princess devoted much time and thought to how she would like her baby to be brought up. 'Normal' was the word she used. 'I want my children to lead ordinary lives,' she insisted – as Eileen Parker, ex-wife of Philip's equerry, told me. But normal and ordinary were exactly what the royal family were not. Nor had they been noticeable characteristics of Philip's upbringing. Both he and Elizabeth were the products of distinctly abnormal backgrounds, which had an inevitable effect on the way that they each approached parenthood.

The future Queen, like all her immediate relations, had been raised by nannies. Self-sacrificing, hard-working Scottish women from modest backgrounds were charged with the responsibility of turning out well-mannered, well-behaved princes and princesses. Some were brutal in their methods – Elizabeth's father George VI and his brothers were abused by one nursery maid – but most were kind and affectionate surrogate mothers who loved their charges and whose only practical reward was the hugs and kisses they received in return.

Princess Elizabeth had been looked after by Clara Knight, who had been nurse to the Princess's own mother. Known as Alah – a childish derivation of Clara – she adhered to a strict, no-nonsense routine, where everything had a set time and place. Elizabeth's contact with her father and mother was carefully prescribed. She saw them in the morning and the evening, and that was about it. The Duke and Duchess of York were determined that they were not going to be subjected to the rigours and restrictions that had made the Duke's own childhood an unmitigated misery, but that did not extend to building their own lives around their daughter. When she was only nine months old, Elizabeth's mother left her in the care of her nanny while the Duchess joined her husband on a six-month tour of Australia.

Leaving her baby behind was tough for the Duchess of York, but surprisingly, Queen Mary took quite an interest in her role as a grandmother, which she shared with Lady Strathmore. The Duchess of York wrote to her mother-in-law that she missed her daughter 'quite terribly' and that 'the five weeks we have been away seem like five months'. Queen Mary's replies to her daughter-in-law conveyed a warmth that she rarely displayed in person as she described the baby's delight in watching her husband's parrot Charlotte make her flat-footed way across the break-fast table to crack an egg with her beak or eat fruit pips.

She also wrote to her son, Bertie, describing how the 'adorable child' would shriek with delight 'at each dog she saw'.

History was to repeat itself when Princess Elizabeth and Prince Philip left on their tour of the Commonwealth, which took them away for six months, when Prince Charles was just five years old. Even before that, they travelled to Canada and the USA, missing Charles's third birthday. Forced absences were part of the strictures of being royal in the '50s, and although tours are far shorter today, royal children still have to take second place.

Although Clarence House was being prepared (with a generous government grant of £50,000 for its refurbishment) as the marital home for Elizabeth and Philip, who had become the Duke and Duchess of Edinburgh on their marriage, it was not yet ready when Charles was born. Prince Philip had taken great interest in every detail of the plans and took every opportunity to see how things were getting on, driving into London in his MG sports car at breakneck speed to check out the progress on their future home. They were not homeless, however, as in addition to an apartment in Buckingham Palace, they leased a large country house, Windlesham Moor near Bagshot in Surrey, where they spent weekends entertaining their friends.

The Victorian manor house, now owned by a member of the Al Maktoum family, stood in almost 60 acres but was not grand by royal standards. It had four reception rooms, a hall, a dining room, a 50-foot drawing room and a 'Chinese room'. Other rooms included a study, a games room, loggia and five main bedrooms. The upstairs nursery comprised two guest rooms joined together that were used for some of the half-dozen staff, including the Princess's dresser Bobo and Philip's valet John Dean when the royal couple were in residence. Prince Charles had his own nursery footman, John Gibson, who later penned a memoir of his time in royal service. Gibson reminds us how revered royal children were in the early '50s and describes how he had sole responsibility for the large royal pram, which he had to wash and polish for twenty minutes before Charles's nanny would allow him to take the baby Prince for his daily walk. According to Gibson, the nanny, Helen Lightbody, was 'very strict and very formal' – so much so that he was obliged to refer to the baby as His Royal Highness at all times: 'There would have been real trouble if I had arrived at the nursery door with a tray and said: "Here's Charles's breakfast" or even "Here is Prince Charles's breakfast." I had to remember to say: "I have brought His Royal Highness's breakfast."'

Two world wars had delivered a hammer blow to the cosy, upper-class world of servants and nurseries. The royal family, however, had weathered this development largely unchanged, and Charles soon fell into the routine that had been so much a part of Elizabeth's own childhood. He was taken to see his mother every morning at nine, just as she had been taken to see her parents. And in the evenings, engagements permitting, she would join him in the nursery. But that was just about the extent of it; they lived largely separate lives. 'To my knowledge, she never bathed the children,' recalled Mike Parker's ex-wife Eileen. 'Nanny did all that.'

Charles's birth was seen as a new beginning after the years of war, rationing and unemployment. But two weeks after the infant Prince's birth, an impenetrable fog descended on London and stayed for several days. It caused three train crashes and driving was impossible. Buses and police cars were taken off the road and ambulances stopped functioning, so people had to make their own way to hospital. Londoners wore handkerchiefs wrapped around their faces and were obliged to walk along the pavements armed with a stick or a closed umbrella to feel where the pavement ended and the road began.

The baby was not even allowed into the Buckingham Palace gardens in his large, covered pram (the same one that his mother had been pushed about in twenty-two years before) for fear that the dense, sooty vapours would affect his lungs. The Princess didn't want to even consider the possibility that he might come to any harm; she was enraptured by her baby and wanted to keep him near her at all times. She wrote to her former music teacher, Mabel 'Goosey' Lander, 'the baby is very sweet and we are enormously proud of him' but she was even more impressed by his baby hands: 'They are rather large, but fine with long fingers – quite unlike mine and certainly unlike his father's. It will be interesting to see what they will become. I still find it difficult to believe I have a baby of my own!'

Her joy was to be short-lived as on 23 November, just over a week after her baby's birth, her father suffered a blood clot and had to cancel his proposed tour of Australia, New Zealand and Canada. Although the King's condition rapidly improved, his doctors advised complete rest to avoid surgery. Elizabeth knew that all too soon his responsibilities would inevitably fall upon her slender shoulders and had been told the King would not be well enough to undertake his tour. She wanted to have the christening as soon as possible, while her father was strong enough and before the endless Christmas celebrations for the family and staff began in earnest. The one-month-old Prince Charles was christened His Royal Highness Charles Philip Arthur George of Edinburgh in the Music Room at Buckingham Palace, with windows overlooking the gardens. Just before the birth, the King had issued letters patent granting the title Prince or Princess of the United Kingdom, with the style 'Royal Highness', to the children of the Duke of Edinburgh and Princess Elizabeth, Duchess of Edinburgh. Like his mother before him, Charles was baptised with holy water from the River Jordan, dripped from the Lily Font made for the baptism of Queen Victoria's first child. Baby Charles was dressed in the Honiton lace gown that had been worn at the christenings of all Queen Victoria's children, and after by George VI, his brothers and sister, his nephews and nieces, the Gloucesters and Kents, and by his own two daughters, Elizabeth and Margaret. The gown was used by all the royal children until it was considered too delicate and Angela Kelly, the Queen's dresser, was asked by the Queen to make a replica, first worn in 2008.

In the '40s and '50s, royal christenings were very grand affairs and all the godparents were chosen from family rather than friends. As heir presumptive, Charles was no exception, with his godparents comprising: his grand-father the King; his great-grandmother Queen Mary; his aunt Princess Margaret; his paternal great-grandmother Victoria (Marchioness of Milford Haven); his great-uncle David Bowes-Lyon; Earl Mountbatten's daughter, Lady Brabourne, and his great-uncle Prince George of Greece; and King Haakon of Norway. Of the whole group, Princess Margaret was the youngest and, according to David Bowes-Lyon, the Queen Mother's youngest and favourite brother, the most fun. Prince George was the generous elder brother of Prince Philip's father, Andrew, and had looked after Philip and his sisters throughout their exile in France.

Such an exceptional group deserved something special and were given a sumptuous lunch, after which they looked through Queen Victoria's photo albums to see who the baby resembled. Queen Mary thought it was the Prince Consort, Prince Albert, and no one dared to disagree with her.

That Christmas the whole royal family celebrated at Buckingham Palace for the first time in many years. The King was too weak to travel but was determined to get well enough to continue to perform as many duties as he could and move between his various homes – Windsor, Sandringham and Balmoral.

In July 1949, the Duke and Duchess of Edinburgh finally moved into Clarence House and Prince Charles was ensconced in the pale-blue nursery quarters upstairs. His young life had begun where it would settle many years later, in the one place in the world that represented total security – his grandmother's former London residence.

For eight-month-old Prince Charles, young nanny Mabel Anderson became a haven of security. Throughout his young life, his parents were frequently away and he was brought up to mistrust open displays of affection, even in private. In the rarefied world in which they lived, a delicate kiss on the cheek was considered acceptable but hugging was altogether too foreign, too invasive. They were not alone; most aristocratic families were equally distanced from their offspring. It was not that they didn't care; they just did not embrace life in the same way as we do now. But when the late Diana, Princess of Wales, spoke of how her husband had never received affection from his mother, it wasn't quite true. Elizabeth loved her children and they loved her; she just did not feel the need to be demonstrative with them. Though she was as warm as her own mother, the Queen Mother, had been, she, too, came from a generation who felt no need for overt displays of affection.

When Prince Harry complained that his father lacked warmth, he was not taking into account the social mores of the age into which his father was raised. When Harry was a guest on American actor Dax Shepard's *Armchair Expert* podcast in May 2021, he tried to explain what he felt.

I don't think we should be pointing the finger or blaming anybody, but certainly when it comes to parenting, if I've experienced some form of pain or suffering that perhaps my father or my parents had suffered, I'm going to make sure I break that cycle so that I don't pass it on, basically. There is a lot of generic pain and suffering that gets passed on anyway, so we as parents should be doing the most we can to try and say 'You know what? That happened to me, I'm going to make sure it doesn't happen to you.'

On his father King Charles, Harry said, 'I also know that that's connected to his parents, so that means that he's treating me the way he was treated, which means, how can I change that for my own kids? And well, here I am. I've now moved my whole family to the US. That wasn't the plan.'

Harry also says in his book *Spare* that he never hugged his grandmother, the Queen, although there were many times he would like to have done. He also recalls in the book the moment Charles told him Diana had died:

What I do remember with startling clarity is that I didn't cry. Not one tear.

Pa didn't hug me. He wasn't great at showing his emotions under normal circumstances; how could he be expected to show them in such a crisis? But his hand did once fall on my knee and he said, *It's going to be OK.*

That was quite a lot for him. Fatherly, hopeful, kind. And so very untrue.

But he never forgot that Harry didn't like the dark and gently stroked his face that night until he fell asleep.

Harry wrote that he wanted to hug the Queen when she was tapping her foot as guitarist Brian May played on the roof at a concert in the grounds of Buckingham Palace for the Golden Jubilee in 2002.

I wondered, watching Granny rock out to Brian May, if Pa ever tried? Probably not. When he was five or six, Granny left him, went off on a royal tour lasting several months, and when she returned, she offered him a firm handshake. Which may have been more than he ever got from Grandpa.

Partly due to the way the ghostwriter has interpreted Harry's thoughts and partly because Harry simply doesn't have the intellectual curiosity to take outside influences into account, he failed to understand how rigidly conventional families – especially one as steeped in tradition as the royal family – actually worked. Perhaps King Charles had a valid point when he tried to persuade Diana to bring up her sons according to royal tradition, with the emphasis on decorum rather than on having a good time. Diana was a woman with her own ideas of how to bring up children and she was emphatic that her 'boys', as she called them, should be spared the ruthless, unremitting regulation and discipline that Charles had to endure when he was young and which she believed rendered him incapable of being emotionally open.

Diana may have had a point, but whatever it did or didn't achieve, it enabled Charles to perform the role he was born to and to perform it with seamless style during a period of extreme instability for the whole world.

2

LEARNING HOW

Like many people in their mid-seventies, King Charles complains his memory has become increasingly bad. 'My memory is appalling,' he told me, and he explained that in order to remedy this, he writes down his thoughts on crested paper notelets that fit into the top pocket of his jacket. They are removed by his valet, who passes them on to the appropriate people to action.

Charles can be a demanding boss, though he is never afraid to apologise if he feels he has been hasty or unreasonable to his domestic staff. On one occasion he called his unfortunate valet away from his supper to ask him why he had not unbuttoned the shirt he was about to wear. He is also adamant about the clocks at Highgrove and insists they should all keep precise time. If he notices that one has stopped, he shakes his hands and proclaims, 'My clocks! My clocks! What am I to do?' He then sends a note to the appropriate member of staff, reprimanding them.

If one of the lights above the fine pictures from the Royal

Collection that adorns the walls happens to fail, a memo will be sent to the staff warning against a repeat of such a calamity. If little pieces of gravel are inadvertently brought into the house from the driveway, Charles sends the house-keeper a note and warns it must never happen again, regardless of the possibility it might have been he who was responsible and had simply forgotten.

Considering the enormous number of people Charles has met, and the number of things he does in a day, it would be extraordinary if he could recall much of his childhood in great detail, but his long-term memory is surprisingly good.

One of the first things Charles says he remembers is being in his large pram and thinking how far it was from where he was sitting to the hands holding the rail behind him. It was his third birthday and a film of him being wheeled through Green Park with his nanny and a smart royal-protection officer wearing a '40s homburg hat and long overcoat was shown by Pathé News in cinemas in celebration of the event. He also remembers sitting on a sofa with his grandfather, King George VI, while someone swung 'something shiny' at the end of a chain to hold his attention. The photograph was taken on his third birthday, ostensibly for his parents who were in Canada, but also for the King and Queen's private collection. The photo-graph had pride of place in his mother's sitting room for many years, as it combines almost her last memory of her father and one of the earliest portraits of her son.

In April 1954, at the age of five and a half, Prince Charles and his sister Princess Anne were driven to Portsmouth with their grandmother Queen Elizabeth, their governess Miss Peebles and two nannies, Helen Lightbody and Mabel Anderson. They were off to Malta on the maiden voyage of the newly completed Royal Yacht *Britannia* and then on to Tobruk to meet their parents. They had not seen them since November 1953 as the royal couple had been on a six-month tour of the Commonwealth. Charles and Anne had the time of their young lives on board *Britannia*. There was a sandbox on the upper deck for them to dig in and a pedal car for Charles, and instead of being with their nannies and their governess they played with members of the crew assigned to them. When they arrived in Malta, Charles was far more excited to be taken aboard the aircraft carrier *Eagle* than at the prospect of seeing his mother and father at the next port. It was not until 2 May, when the Queen was piped on board *Britannia* in Tobruk, that Charles saw his mother again. It had been a long six months apart, but Charles was so impressed by the smart naval officers that he had to be dissuaded from joining them in line to salute and shake hands with his mother, rather than hug her.

Despite her reticence towards any kind of public displays of affection (which lasted all her life), the young Queen was obviously excited to see her children again. Prince Charles was a delightful but rather vague, sensitive little boy. His sister Anne was quite the opposite, fearless and brave and far more like her irascible father. Charles formed deep relationships with the women who looked after him during his formative years when his mother was too busy with affairs of state to devote much time to him. Nannies Helen Lightbody and Mabel Anderson, and his governess Miss Peebles – who was known as 'Mipsy' – were the most important women in his life. When Helen Lightbody left royal service in 1956, Charles was distraught, and when she died in a Scottish nursing home aged seventy-nine in 1987, he organised an ornate wreath with a handwritten personal message for her funeral. 'Nana' Lightbody had been with him throughout those formative years now considered so important and championed by the new Princess of Wales. According to Jonathan Dimbleby's official biography of Charles, Nana was apt to remind her charge of his special position and the important duties he had in front of him, which was the very thing Charles's parents were anxious to avoid. Regardless of what his father thought, Charles kept in touch with Nana her whole life, inviting her to his investiture in 1969 and to his twenty-first birthday celebrations.

When Mabel Anderson was put in charge, she turned the nursery floor into her own friendly kingdom. Whenever Charles returned from school, it was to the Buckingham Palace nursery he ran before even seeing his parents. His warm relationship with Mabel Anderson continued until such time as she left the palace and went to work for Princess Anne when Peter Phillips was born. Charles has fond memories from his boyhood years of the nursery with Mabel's Roberts radio tuned into Terry Wogan on Radio 2, and to this day Mabel is a hugely important person in his life. She lives in a grace-and-favour apartment in Frogmore House at Windsor that he had decorated to her specific demands at his own expense.

The Queen always described her young son as 'a country person', and indeed he was. He loved riding the Dartmoor pony that had been presented to his mother and kept at the Royal Mews, and he enjoyed following the shooting parties at Sandringham before he learned to shoot properly. But he adored Balmoral most of all, and it has continued to be his favourite place in the whole world.

It was from Balmoral that Charles took his first-ever plane journey, in an aircraft of the Queen's Flight. In June 1955, after one of the worst late winters on record, when thousands of sheep on hill farms froze to death, Charles and Anne flew from Aberdeen to London. It was the era of rock 'n' roll, and Bill Haley & His Comets had a number-one single with 'Rock Around the Clock', but for Charles and Anne, in their gilded youthful world, nothing could be more thrilling than sitting on their mother's plane with Wing Commander John Crindon as pilot and Sir Edward Fielden, Captain of the Queen's Flight, explaining how everything worked. It was an exciting experience, as they previously travelled back from Balmoral on the Royal Train, and sitting in the cockpit to have a look at the instrument panel was a very special treat for Charles.

A year later, in November 1956, Prince Charles, accompanied by his governess Miss Peebles, was driven to Hill House School in Knightsbridge to begin his schooldays. He was the first heir to the throne to go to school at such a young age, let alone to a day school. His parents had at least taken the trouble to let him approach his schooldays gently by employing a young tutor, Michael Farebrother, a former Grenadier Guards officer and head of a small school, St Peter's at Seaford in Sussex, over the Christmas holidays. Christmas that year was spent at Sandringham, and Farebrother played football with Charles, went bike-riding with him and accompanied him on expeditions to nearby Brancaster beach. More importantly, he was there to explain what to expect when he found himself no longer the centre of a world dominated by nannies and govern-esses but among 120 boisterous boys. It wasn't the greatest start for Charles as he was constantly unwell, missing days at a time. But the other boys were kind to him and he was never bullied. He has no particular memory of his time there except that it was much nicer than any of the schools he attended afterwards. Being such a self-contained boy and something of a dreamer, it was clear that Charles was not cut out for traditional school life.

In 1958, the last term of his first year at his prep school Cheam, Charles was in his headmaster's study at school, watching the closing ceremony of the Commonwealth Games in Cardiff with some other boys, when his mother's voice came over the speakers announcing, 'I intend to create my son, Charles, Prince of Wales today.' There was a thunder of applause and then hundreds of Welsh voices sang 'God Bless the Prince of Wales'. When the crowd fell silent, the Queen continued: 'When he is grown up, I will present him to you at Caernarfon.' The experience remained in his memory because he says it was the moment it dawned on him – 'the awful fate' that lay in store. In acquiring the title, he automatically became a Knight of the Garter and the other rollcall of titles that go with being heir apparent to the English and Scottish throne: Earl of Chester, Duke of Cornwall, Duke of Rothesay, Earl of Carrick, Lord of the Isles and Baron Renfrew, Prince and Great Steward of Scotland, Knight Companion of the Most Noble Order of the Garter. He was nine years and eight months old.

The tragedy was that his mother had not told him what she was going to say or indeed that she was going to say it. The Queen was not physically present at the Commonwealth Games as she had painful sinus trouble and was obliged to record the message rather than make the pronouncement in person. Later she came to regard the declamation, dropped on an unsuspecting child, as one of the few mistakes she made in Charles's upbringing. Peter Beck, then headmaster of Cheam School, later remembered the outward look of trepidation on Charles's face. Charles recalled the inner turmoil: 'I remember being acutely embarrassed when it was announced,' he said. 'I heard a marvellous great cheer coming from the stadium in Cardiff and I think for a little boy of nine it was bewildering. All the others turned and looked at me in amazement.'

When he was still at Cheam, Prince Charles's acting talent had its first real airing when he played the ill-fated Duke of Gloucester in a play entitled *The Last Baron*. The play was Cheam School's adaptation of Shakespeare's *Richard III* and the Prince got to play the future King when the leading actor suddenly left the school. He was complimented on his performance and style in the *Cheam Chronicle* and the experience encouraged his love of Shakespeare and his ability to deliver his words as well as he does today in many of his speeches.

On the final night of the play, the headmaster stepped onto the stage to announce that the Queen had just given birth to a second son, Prince Andrew. Again, it was terribly embarrassing for the eleven-year-old Prince and, although he was excited and happy about the baby, it was yet another moment during his childhood when he was made to feel different and awkward. At least his mother had not been able to come and see the play because of her condition, thus sparing him any blushes over the ensuing fuss that would invariably have been made had she arrived at the school. It was a big event for the home-loving Charles to have a baby brother. As soon as he was back at Buckingham Palace, he spent most of his spare time in the nursery with nanny Mabel Anderson and the infant Prince Andrew. Charles himself once said that sometimes a whole day and night would pass before he went to see his mother or she asked to see him.

It was the nursery that provided Charles with the only real love and security he would know. But even that sanctuary was not sacrosanct. Nanny Lightbody's disagreements with Prince Philip came to a head, and when Charles came home from school one day the surrogate mother he had loved so much had been summarily 'retired'.

By the standards of the '50s, Charles was an extremely

privileged little boy. He had his own pony; he had been on the maiden voyage of his mother's very own superyacht, *Britannia*, and been assigned his own midshipman to look after him, had his own pedal car on board and had been given the latest child-friendly camera with which to try to take pictures. He had flown in a private plane from Scotland to London and had his own bedroom and bathroom aboard his own carriage in the Royal Train. By the standards of some of the billionaires today it may not seem much, but in the United Kingdom's austerity of the post-war years, it was extraordinary.

Charles was very much loved by both his parents, but they were distant. They seldom hugged him, as neither of them were tactile people, apart from the usual kisses good-night. It did not mean they didn't love him, but they did not feel any necessity to show or vocalise their feelings. It is the unique and curious way the upper and upper-middle classes brought up their children, who came to rely on Nanny for affection. Nanny also acted as a buffer between the parents and children, and throughout Princes William and Harry's childhood any hint of a parental row would see the boys whisked away by one of their two nannies. If Nanny was not there for some reason, there was a house-keeper and two protection officers on hand. Certainly, Prince Harry did not observe any unpleasantness from his parents, although William, being two years older, some-times heard his parents fighting and witnessed Diana's tearful outbursts.

In his livestream chat with controversial trauma therapist

Gabor Maté, Harry claimed that he came from a broken home and was a 'boy in a bubble' because of the environment he was 'confined' in. Speaking of fatherhood, he said he wanted to avoid the emotional distance that defined his relationship with his own father – recalling again how Charles broke the news of Diana's death to him without hugging him. All of which is probably true – to Harry, anyway – but what he failed to understand was that his father was a product of his time and never loved Harry any less because of it.

There were plenty of instances when father and son spent many happy hours together when Harry was young and he was learning about nature and plants. 'Plants have feelings too,' Charles explained to Harry, and he described how he talked to his plants to encourage their growth. Charles's way of loving his sons was to teach them to enjoy the things he enjoyed, rather than smothering them. Harry explained he 'bombards' his own children with the love he feels he never received from his own father.

The Queen may not have prepared Charles for life with tactile love in the way one would do with a child today, but in a different way she felt Prince Charles had to be gently introduced to his future role. So, everything she and Prince Philip did was in some way preparation for him to take over the job she had inherited at the age of twenty-five, after the death of her father. The Queen decided that as five-year-old Charles was a shy, retiring child, he would benefit from the solo teachings of a governess, rather than being with other royal children in the Buckingham Palace schoolroom, and so he began his education with Miss Peebles. If the Queen had had her way, she would have continued to have him educated at home. Prince Philip had decidedly different ideas. He was insistent that, once the elementary period of his education under Miss Peebles had been completed, Charles would be sent away to school. 'The Queen and I want Charles to go to school with other boys of his generation to learn to live with other children and to absorb from childhood the discipline imposed by education with others,' Prince Philip explained during a visit to the USA in 1956.

Given the benefit of hindsight and considering the social changes that have taken place in the intervening years, it is difficult to see what other decision the Queen and Prince Philip could have arrived at. But it was tough for Charles, and the Queen, wary of something she had not experienced herself, continued to harbour reservations.

Charles was sent to Cheam School, his father's old prep school, in Hampshire. The Queen remembered him shuddering with terror on the journey there. For nights after she left him, he cried himself to sleep – quietly, into his pillow, hopeful that no one would hear him – in his wooden bed, which, as his mother had observed before she left him, looked too hard to jump on. The memory still hurt, Charles said many years later, declaring it one of the unhappiest times of his life. No matter how hard he tried to mingle with the other pupils, Charles always stood out. He had never had to fend for himself, never learned to fight his corner, had never travelled on a bus or been into a shop and knew nothing of money except that his mother's head was on the coins. He had never had the opportunity to learn how to make friends with people of his own age and he was inevitably singled out by both his teachers and his contemporaries. It was the same on the sports field; Charles was not a team player. He much preferred the safety and comfort of the palace, but once away at school, that lifeline of security was broken. Charles hated it.

Charles felt the separation from his family very deeply. He dreaded going away to school. He was used to the coddled security of nannies and nursery maids – now, suddenly, he was on his own. No Mabel, no Granny or sister, no Mipsy and, however distant, no Mother. 'He would write to Mipsy every day,' Princess Anne recalled. 'He was heartbroken. He used to cry into his letters and say, "I miss you".' The governess was equally distressed by the absence of the little boy she had come to love. She stayed on to teach Anne and then Andrew, and she and Charles corresponded with one another until she died.

Mipsy passed away in her apartment in the impersonal vastness of Buckingham Palace over a weekend in 1968, and her body was not found until more than forty-eight hours later, when a footman came to her rooms. The royal family and their staff were deeply shocked that such a gentle woman should come to such a tragic end and at a relatively young age. Charles was inconsolable when he was told the news. Mipsy had been with them for fifteen years and was closer to Charles than his own mother. It was the first time in his young life that someone he cared for so much had been taken away from him and he took a long time to get over it.

Charles was lonely. Not at home, where he had the serenity of the nursery and the full support system of nannies and female relations to service him with the necessary emotional succour – which, had his temperament been of a different kind, might have been enough to see him through. M. Scott Peck, an American psychologist who wrote *The Road Less Traveled* (1978), a timeless classic in personal development that has sold over 5 million copies, claimed that we tend to project onto the world what our childhood home was like. Children who grow up in nurturing homes tend to see the world as a warm, nurturing place, and those that grow up in a home filled with hostility tend to see the world as a cold, hostile and dangerous place.

Charles could see the resentment his regal position generated in those around him. He may have seen less of his mother than he would have liked and there were moments of tension with his father, but his home was still full of joy, from both the family and the staff. At school it was different. He had to be forced to make any friends at all. The maths master at Cheam, David Munir, who had been delegated to keep an eye on him, recalled seeing Charles standing apart from the general throng of boys, bewildered and frightened. Charles was denied the friendship of what he called the 'nicest' boys, who did not wish to appear to be sucking up to him. This problem beset him throughout his schooldays and beyond, until he was old enough to retreat behind the protective wall of his position and only mix with those he chose to, not those with whom chance had thrown him into contact.

'Shyness,' Charles later observed, drawing from his own pitiable experience at the time, 'is often a disability. It isn't only those who are confined to a wheelchair who are disabled.'

Before Charles was sent to Cheam, the Queen had invited the headmasters of a number of suitable prep schools to some of the informal lunches at Buckingham Palace that Prince Philip instituted in the summer of 1956 as a method of meeting people she might not otherwise ever have encountered. None of them presented as good a case for their establishment as Philip did for his old school and, without the Queen ever having met Cheam's joint headmasters, it was decided Charles would follow in his father's educational footsteps, which was then the British way. 'Then,' said Prince Philip, 'there is no further argument.'

The decision to send Charles to Gordonstoun, the senior school founded in Scotland by Kurt Hahn and attended by Philip as one of the founder pupils, was not quite so easily won. The Queen Mother, for one, was keen for her sensitive grandson to go to Eton College near Windsor, where generations of kings and princes had been educated. The former Queen Empress was not used to her wishes being ignored and wrote to her daughter begging her to intervene and keep the 'sensitive and creative' boy closer to home, but much to her annoyance it was to no avail. 'He will feel terribly cut off and lonely in the far north,' she told her daughter in one letter. 'I suppose he will be taking his entrance exam for Eton soon. I do hope he passes because it might be the ideal school for one of his character and temperament.'

The Queen knew nothing about the world of schools, especially boys' schools, except that Charles had hated his first year at Cheam and only began to enjoy it when the end was in sight. She was wary of Eton, because it was just over the bridge from Windsor Castle and she knew he would be watched and followed by reporters and photographers even more than he had been at Cheam. Charles was anxious to go to Charterhouse in Surrey, where some of his friends were going, but was overruled by Philip, who strongly felt Charles would benefit not only from the location of Gordonstoun but from its forward-thinking education and spartan environment.

The Queen Mother, too, was overruled, and Philip won the day, as the Queen knew he would. Buckingham Palace released a formal note to the Fleet Street papers, thanking them for finally leaving Charles alone to continue his education at Cheam. They hoped what they called 'this happy state of affairs' would continue during his stay at Gordonstoun because 'Her Majesty and His Royal Highness felt he will only be able to derive full benefit from his days at school if he is not made the centre of special attention.'

Being the centre of special attention – other than when he was on stage – was what Charles hated. He wanted to be just like everyone else, which is what children of his age the world over want, regardless of their situation. But for Charles there was no getting away from the fact that being the centre of attention was what his future was all about. After Prince Philip had left the timid and embarrassed Charles at his new school, instead of driving away like all the other parents, he went to join the headmaster for lunch. He was then chauffeured to collect his aircraft at Lossiemouth, which he piloted himself, flying low over the school and giving Charles a farewell tilt of the wings as he flew off. How to get a new boy noticed. Charles was mortified.

The Gordonstoun of Charles's time was not as tough as some legend suggests. The cold showers of the '60s were never more than a quick run-through and were always preceded by much longer, hotter ones. The early morning run was no more than a 45-yard jog up the road, and then only if it was not raining, but it was still tough enough – as former pupil Ross Benson, who was in Charles's house, Windmill Lodge, and the same class, recalled.

The 'torture', as we knew it, would take place every morning at 7.20 am unless there was a thick frost on the ground. Prince Charles would come out with the rest of us dressed in white shorts and plimsols, stumbling and half asleep. Tracksuits were not allowed, and within minutes we were blue with cold. Afterwards we all made a dash for the hot showers – you had to be quick, as there were sixty boys and only fifteen showers. Quite often Charles got left behind. He would then go off in his regulation dressing gown and wait until it was his turn to have a shower. You had to have a cold shower after the hot one and it was strictly illegal to miss it as some did, but not Charles.

Nobody else in the school had a father who arrived in a helicopter to see his son, as Prince Philip did on more than one occasion. Poor Charles tried to cover his embarrassment when this happened and obviously wished the ground would swallow him up. On one of these visits, Charles proudly showed his father his pottery and was able to present his mother with a vase he made in the school pottery sessions. In fact, he made her six vases; he did have some help with the glaze from teacher Mr Waddell, but the basic pattern was his idea. His favourite piece had a bold sunflower design and it won him a silver award at the school's annual art show.

On another occasion, when Charles, his detective Donald Green and some of the boys were out on a camping expedition, one of the party, Alistair Dobson, was given the task of going to ask the local farmer if they could buy some milk. Dobson knocked on the door of the only farmhouse in sight, nearly a mile away, and was told by the farmer there was no milk for sale. Dobson returned shamefaced and admitted he'd had no luck. Without saying anything, Charles got up and went off himself to see what he could do. He later told Alistair Dobson the tale:

I knocked on the door, just like you did – the farmer came to the door and started telling me off for disturbing him again and he had no milk for sale. Suddenly he recognised who I was and stopped mid-sentence. He turned red and went into a sort of funny fit of blinking, and after muttering an apology returned with two pints of milk which I tried to pay for, after thanking him profusely. He looked completely flabbergasted and even his wife came to the front door to see me off. My money was refused. You see, there are some advantages of having your photograph in the papers. People recognise you – useful when you need milk!

The boys all burst out laughing and according to Charles, his parents and admiring younger brother laughed a lot when he told them in the holidays.

Charles always felt unhappy with the awe with which some masters surrounded him at Gordonstoun and the faintly imbecilic way in which people who caught sight of him from outside the school used to stare when he passed by. If he didn't want to answer something, he would just ignore it. Boys would try hard to provoke him, hoping that discussing his family loud enough for him to hear would get a rise out of him: 'The best thing would be to get Charles to invite you home during the holidays, meet Anne and have her marry you. Then you will have no problems at all.' Charles scowled but said nothing. He would have been justified in punching the boy, but he never did lose control and he never got involved in a schoolboy fight.

At rugby he would often stand with his hands behind

his back, his thoughts miles away. Boys from the other houses who were due to play his team that day would love the idea of having a go at Charles. The attitude was, *'I'm going to hammer him today.'* It did not mean there was any personal malice towards Charles; it was just that here was the future King of England, and the thought of pushing his face into the mud of Scotland was too inviting to be missed, as Ross Benson recalled:

> I remember one boy telling me: 'I tackled Charles good and hard today. It was right in the middle of a muddy patch and I pushed his nose right into the muck.' But if his tough treatment upset Charles, he never showed it openly and never complained at the personal attention he received. Even when he broke his nose in a particularly rough game he never 'squealed' nor did he make any sort of protest.

Charles was courageous as, despite the bullying on the rugby field, he continued to play right up to the time he left Gordonstoun. He played as a lock forward and when it came to his turn to tackle, he never hesitated, nor did he show any signs of fear.

While Charles tried hard to hide his deep feelings for his mother – something which all schoolboys attempt to do for fear of being thought 'sissies' – there was no hiding his pleasure whenever she came to the school. Surprisingly, she too dropped her regal mask when seeing Charles. Benson remembered:

On one occasion, a special service was heard in Michael Kirk, a tiny chapel. Charles had written to his mother inviting her to attend and she made a special journey north, and she came into the chapel with her son who was holding her arm. We were already in position before they entered, and no one could help but notice their enjoyment at being reunited. The Queen sat next to Charles and they whispered together quite often between bouts of organ playing. Talking during the service is not allowed in church but of course we were all too polite and pretended we didn't notice rules being broken.

In his last year at Gordonstoun, Charles was chosen to play the Pirate King in *The Pirates of Penzance*, the comic opera by Gilbert and Sullivan. He hadn't the faintest trace of nerves on the opening night and sang 'It is a glorious thing to be a Pirate King!'. The audience burst out laughing, but Charles did not falter and went on singing as if nothing had happened.

When the Queen came up to see the play, she smiled with delight when she heard the last lines: 'We yield at once, with humbled mien, because, with all our faults, we love our Queen.'

Ross Benson recollected:

Both Charles and I were members of Sophists Club, a debating society which met every Wednesday evening at the home of deputy English master, Eric Anderson [later headmaster, then provost of Eton, who became a good friend of Prince Charles]. We crammed into detective Michael Varney's Land Rover and drove to Anderson's sixteenth-century house next to Elgin Cathedral.

Politeness and a complete lack of aggression are the principal impressions Charles left at the school – but when he got up to speak in a debate, all the shyness and reserve dropped from Charles like a cloak, and he was one of the best debaters in the Sophists. His views, if sometimes rather illogical, were always well put. He would sit down with the notes on his knee, or he would stand with his hands behind his back, and the moment he spoke, authority would creep into his voice and his bearing. The subjects were 'Are we becoming too materialistic a society?' or 'Are computers dehumanizing us?' The subject of the monarchy was strictly taboo.

Normally Charles had middle-of-the-road views and was never extreme about anything. He prepared his speeches diligently, but there were none of the quick flashes of inspired thought for which his father was famous. On the other hand, he was convincing and commanded respect.

One of the rare occasions Charles blossomed occurred during the mock elections at the school, held just before a General Election. Charles took the role of a vociferous supporter of the Scottish Nationalists and, wearing his Stewart kilt, marched up and down the grounds shouting, 'Scotland for ever!', 'Freedom for the Scots and down with rule from Whitehall!' Together with his other political supporters, he held aloft large banners reading: 'Vote for the Scottish Nationalists'.

Charles made vigorous election speeches backing his party. He was once heckled by a Tory supporter who reminded him that he was a Prince of Wales and not a Prince of Scotland. This left Charles nonplussed, but only for a moment and he quickly recovered and retaliated: 'Freedom for Wales, too. That is for the next election,' amid laughter.

Charles had a deep love for the Scottish countryside. He was fond of wearing his kilt whenever he could and when the Queen came to see him on his last day at school, he commemorated the occasion by wearing the Hunting Stewart kilt. He was also very fond of reading Scottish poetry, and Robert Burns was one of his favourites. He had a book of Scottish ballads that he often carried around with him. Charles learned tracts of poetry off by heart and was never happier than when he went off fishing by himself with a book of ballads or Shakespeare sonnets in his pocket.

When Charles got on the stage his lack of nerves was even more pronounced, especially in his final year, when he played the leading role in *Macbeth*. He was impressively calm, especially given that the stage jutted out into the hall and the audience were seated on both sides of the actors who appeared directly in their midst. The Queen and Prince Philip flew up to Scotland to see their son's performance and Charles did not falter once, even when his father burst out laughing in the middle of a scene. 'I had to lie on a huge fur rug and have a nightmare,' he explained to a group of actors in 2002. He recounted how, as he thrashed about under the spotlight with the audience on either side, 'all I could hear was my father and "Ha, ha, ha." I went up to him at the end and said: "Why did you laugh?" and he said: "It sounds like The Goons".'

One thing Charles was suspicious of was social functions. When a party of twenty-five girls were invited to a dance at Gordonstoun, Charles went off to spend the weekend with his grandmother at Birkhall, her house on the Balmoral estate. The girls stayed overnight and played tennis the next morning, but although Charles was keen on tennis, he didn't reappear until well after the girls had departed. Even those in his class, such as Ross Benson, who invited him to parties in the holidays, were rebuffed.

> Charles could have had as many girlfriends as he wanted, and even the school maids would stare and giggle amongst themselves if they saw him. They also had a penchant for purloining his underwear, and after the disappearance of some of his clothes sent for washing, there were special precautions taken to ensure that nothing marked with his name would ever get 'lost' again.

On one occasion, one of the senior boys had the bright idea of making a tape recording of Prince Charles snoring. Waiting until he was asleep, several boys crept up to the open window of Charles's dormitory – by Gordonstoun regulations, windows were always kept wide open – and lowered the microphone by an extension cable to just above his head. It was easy enough to do, for Charles's bed was right under the window.

The plan worked like a charm and a little later that night the excited plotters listened gleefully to the loud snores of the future King on their tape recorder. But alas, Charles's housemaster heard about it and confiscated the tape. However, one boy swore he had made a second tape recording, taken from the original on his own machine. If so, someone today, somewhere, has a tape recording of King Charles snoring.

3

ANCESTRY

The royal family's reign as monarchs spans thirty-seven generations and 1,209 years in an unbroken chain, except for the Interregnum period during which Oliver Cromwell served as Lord Protector of England, Scotland and Ireland from 1653 until his death in 1658. 'The Commonwealth of England', as it was called, was a republic that replaced the monarchy after the execution of King Charles I in 1649, and it lasted until the restoration of the monarchy in 1660, when Charles II was crowned king.

The monarchy are descendants of King Alfred the Great, who reigned from 871 to 899 and is considered the first Anglo-Saxon king. Both Queen Elizabeth II and King Charles III come from a long line of nobility and have hundreds of ancestors from various royal 'houses' in history, such as the houses of Stuart, Tudor and Hanover. Royal houses change when there is a succession problem, such as the absence of an heir or when a new dynasty comes to power through conquest or marriage. For example, the Stuart dynasty ended with Queen Anne, who died in 1714 without any surviving heirs. The Hanoverian dynasty then ascended to the throne through the Act of Settlement of 1701, which designated Sophia, Electress of Hanover, heir to the throne. The current British royal family, the House of Windsor, was established in 1917 when King George V changed the name of the royal house from the German-sounding 'Saxe-Coburg and Gotha' (from Queen Victoria's husband Albert's house) to 'Windsor', due to anti-German sentiment during the First World War.

After Princess Elizabeth married Lieutenant Philip Mountbatten RN, the House of Windsor might have come to an end on the death of King George VI. Philip's uncle, Dickie Mountbatten, an arrogant and highly ambitious man, was heard boasting at dinner parties that the royal family name would in due course become the House of Mountbatten. When this was reported to George VI's mother, Queen Mary, she was appalled. Queen Elizabeth, later known as the Queen Mother, persuaded her husband King George VI to intervene with the assistance of the government. The Cabinet agreed that Windsor was to remain the family name. Prince Philip was so incensed at not being able to give his name to his children that he complained that 'I am nothing but a bloody amoeba. I am the only man in the country not allowed to give his name to his own children.' A compromise was eventually agreed whereby descendants of the Queen and Prince Philip who do not have their own royal title, such as Prince or Princess, would have the name Mountbatten-Windsor.

For hundreds of years the family trees of the royal houses of Europe showed a high degree of intermarriage: cousins married cousins, princes and princesses never married commoners and large families were the norm. Queen Victoria and her German husband Prince Albert had nine children, who in turn produced twenty-eight grandchildren. Their marriages linked the far-reaching powers of Great Britain, Germany and Russia and kept the royal blood flowing in their veins. King George VI's marriage to Lady Elizabeth Bowes-Lyon would make him the first English monarch for 300 years who had not married royalty. Although Elizabeth was the aristocratic daughter of an earl, she was considered a commoner. When Prince Charles married Lady Diana Spencer, she was also perceived to be a commoner. When Prince William married Catherine Middleton, who did not have a title of any kind, she too was deemed a commoner. By the time their son Prince George eventually succeeds to the throne, the royal blue blood will have become a mere trickle.

Any doctor will confirm that royal blood is no different from anyone else's blood. Genes, however, are an entirely different matter. They contain information for making specific molecules and proteins that allow human cells to function and control how the body grows and operates. Genes also contain the material that results in particular physical characteristics and traits, like the colour of hair and eyes. Every individual has their own specific DNA, which contains strands of their ancestors' genes. Theoretically, these genes can continue for an infinite number of generations, as long as the genetic material is properly replicated and passed on to the next generation.

With this transmission of DNA, there have been some notable genetic conditions that have affected members of the royal family throughout history. For example, haemophilia, a bleeding disorder caused by a deficiency in clotting factors, was present in the royal family due to a mutation in the X chromosome carried by Queen Victoria, who passed it on to several of her descendants, including her son Leopold and her grandson Alexei, the son of Nicholas II of Russia. It was because he claimed he could cure Alexei's haemophilia that Grigori Rasputin, the mystic and sexual deviant, was able to exercise influence and a degree of control over the Russian royal family.

In 2013, a skeleton found under a car park in Leicester was identified as the bones of King Richard III. Richard was portrayed as deformed by Tudor historians and the skeleton's spine was badly curved, giving the appearance of a hunchback. The bones were of a man in his late twenties or early thirties; Richard was thirty-two when he died. His skeleton had suffered multiple injuries, including eight to the skull at around the time of death. Genetic testing through his maternal DNA proved conclusively that the body was that of Richard III, who was killed at the Battle of Bosworth Field in 1485. Because Richard was childless, scientists looked at the descendants of Edward III, his great-great-grandfather. Fathers pass on a copy of certain genes to their sons, so Richard and Edward should carry some of the same DNA.

However, when the male line was checked – the descendants of Henry Somerset, the 5th Duke of Beaufort – the DNA did not match Richard's, meaning that at some point in history an adulterous affair had broken the paternal chain. In other words, someone was unknowingly illegitimate. Although it is impossible to say when the affair happened, if it occurred around the time of Edward III (1312–1377) it could call into question whether kings such as Henry VI, Henry VII and Henry VIII had royal blood and, therefore, the right to rule. Without his claim to royalty, it is unlikely Henry VII would have been able to raise an army for the Battle of Bosworth, in which Richard III was killed, and the history of England could have been very different. After the positive identification, the remains of Richard III were interred at Leicester Cathedral in March 2015. The Archbishop of Canterbury led the service, at which Queen Elizabeth II was represented by the Countess of Wessex and she sent a message describing the occasion as 'an event of great national and international significance'.

Queen Elizabeth II's royal lineage goes back centuries. The Queen was the great-granddaughter of Edward VII, who inherited the crown from his mother, Queen Victoria. Through Victoria, as well as several other of her great-great-grandparents, Elizabeth was directly descended on the male side from many monarchs from the House of Stuart (from Mary, Queen of Scots, Robert the Bruce and earlier Scottish royal houses), from the House of Tudor and earlier English royal houses stretching back as far as the seventh-century House of Wessex. As a great-great-granddaughter of Queen

Victoria, she was related to the heads of most of the other European royal houses. Through her great-grandmother Queen Alexandra, she is also descended from the Danish Royal House of Schleswig-Holstein-Sonderburg-Glücksburg, as is Prince Philip and his father Prince Andrew of Greece. The Queen and Prince Philip were third cousins, both being great-great-grandchildren of Queen Victoria.

King Charles III can claim even closer connections to royalty than his mother. Unlike Queen Elizabeth II, whose mother was a commoner, King Charles has royal blood from both parents. Philip's royal antecedents connected him to the highest ranks of European royalty. His bloodlines provide direct links to British royalty, to the Royal House of Denmark, to the Grand Dukes of Hesse in Germany and to the Imperial House of the Romanovs in Russia.

King Charles's great-grandmother, Queen Mary, was royal by birth (her great-grandfather was King George III). Despite being a princess of the German Duchy of Teck, she was born and raised in England. She was first engaged to marry Prince Albert Victor, the eldest son of King Edward VII and her second cousin once removed, but after Albert's sudden death in 1892, Mary agreed to marry his brother, the future King George V. The couple married in 1893 and had six children, two of whom would become reigning monarchs. She died in 1953, one year after her son, King George VI.

Prince Philip's connections to Russia should not be overlooked. His grandfather, King George I of Greece, married the Grand Duchess Olga, a cousin of the Romanovs, giving

Philip a Russian grandmother. King George's sister, Marie, married Tsar Alexander III, and Philip's two aunts, Marie and Alexandra, both married Russian Grand Dukes. His uncle Nicholas married Grand Duchess Ellen of Russia, and his great-aunt Alix (Alexandra Romanov) married Tsar Nicholas II, both of whom were executed along with their children at Ekaterinburg in 1918. Philip's great-aunt Ella, who was the widow of Grand Duke Sergei and the inspiration for Philip's mother Alice's life of service to others, suffered a more horrible death. Also in 1918, she and five other members of the Russian imperial family were thrown down a mine and left to die.

This family closeness explains why Philip was able to help solve a mystery. In the 1990s, Philip allowed British and Russian researchers to test his DNA in order to identify remains found buried in a wood suspected to be those of the Tsarina Alexandra and three of her children, murdered in 1918. After the fall of the Soviet Union, the newly formed Russian Federation government allowed the bodies to be exhumed. As Alexandra's great-nephew, Philip had some of the same DNA as that found in the remains, and the bodies were identified. The test was repeated, with the same result, when the two other children's remains were found nearby.

In 1957, Philip was asked in an interview if he would like to visit the Soviet Union. He replied: 'I would like to go to Russia very much – although the bastards murdered half my family.' All was apparently forgiven in 1994, when Philip joined the Queen on a state visit to Russia at the invitation of President Boris Yeltsin. The couple stayed at the Kremlin during their three-day visit. In a link with history, Philip and the Queen sat in the Tsar's box at the Bolshoi Theatre on their first night, to watch a performance of the ballet *Giselle*. They also spent two days in St Petersburg, where they visited the Hermitage Museum and the palatial quarters of the tsars.

Philip's bloodlines were apparent from his appearance, demeanour and strength of character. His blond hair and deep-blue eyes hint at his Nordic Viking roots; his self-discipline, iron will and work ethic can be attributed to his German ancestry; his abundant sense of humour is Anglo-Saxon; while it is distinctly Russian not to display emotion in public, something that Philip did extremely rarely.

While monarchs over the centuries have had differing attributes and faults, there is one element of common ground that almost all have displayed, and that is a love for horses. The late Queen took a particular joy in all things equine; she bred thoroughbreds at the royal stud, owned racehorses and still rode out with her stud groom of almost thirty years, Terry Pendry, some nine months after being advised to give up riding for the sake of her health. In fact, she had her very last ride aged ninety-six on her fell pony Emma, before leaving for Scotland, where she died in the summer of 2022.

Life at both Balmoral and Sandringham revolved around horses, guns and fishing, and it would have been strange if Charles had turned his back on an inheritance established by his great-great-great grandmother at Balmoral and by her son, Charles's great-great-grandfather Edward VII, at Sandringham. Horses dominate the ceremonial aspect of royal life, for pleasure and for sport, and it would have been unthinkable for Charles not to have become a proficient rider, huntsman and polo player.

The late Queen's interest in horses started when her father, then the Duke of York, kept a hunting box and rode to hounds during the season. As soon as she could walk, Princess Elizabeth would visit the horses in the stables. Her first horse was a Shetland pony called Peggy, given to her by her grandfather King George V as a fourth birthday present. After her first pony, the Queen continued to ride and made her debut as a princess at the annual Trooping the Colour ceremony in 1947, riding side-saddle on a horse named Tommy. From 1969 to 1986 the Queen would ride her horse Burmese for royal ceremonies. Burmese was a black mare that was a gift from the Royal Canadian Mounted Police. In the 1981 Trooping parade, the Queen was praised for her steady hands on the reins of Burmese when the horse was spooked by someone in the crowd who fired blanks from a pistol at them both.

The Queen had a favourite horse, called Sanction, who she rode for many years. As Terry Pendry explained, the horse was 'almost telepathic and had a very strong bond with Her Majesty. He would almost know what the Queen wanted and which direction she would like to go before instructed to do so.' Sanction died in the autumn of 2002 at the age of twenty-four and was buried in Home Park at

Windsor Castle, where all the late Queen's favourite horses were interred. Sanction was the last home-bred horse that the Queen rode before making the decision to ride native fell ponies, who were a little nearer to the ground.

Even after the Queen's mobility problems arose in 2022, she continued to attend the Royal Windsor Horse Show where she had watched Princes Philip take part in the carriage driving competitions. When Prince Philip had to give up polo because of his arthritis and took up carriage driving, the Queen provided him with fell ponies that she bred at her stud on the Balmoral estate.

The Queen's attention to detail in everything equine was legendary, as Terry Pendry explained: 'She could analyse the footfall of a horse and its action, and predict what ground it would be best suited to run on. She even used to look at the way the grass had been cut and rolled on a racecourse, away or against the way the horse was to race. That's detail!' He added: 'If she were a horse, she would be matriarch of the herd. She is fearless. Her Majesty is so wise and knowledgeable about all things equine. She has passed this on through her genes.'

It is well known that those genes have been passed on to her daughter, the Princess Royal, and her granddaughter Zara Tindall, both of whom are Olympic riders. But until the King and Queen hosted the Royal Procession on all five days of Royal Ascot in the year of their coronation, many imagined the King was not as interested in horses as his late mother. Charles would never claim to have anything like the late Queen's knowledge of horses or to be as good a rider as his sister, but with the encouragement of Camilla, on inheriting his mother's considerable equine collection he has become a serious fan.

King Charles has ridden since he was a child and although he was never as competitive as Princess Anne, made his debut as an amateur jockey at the age of thirty-one, in a charity race at Plumpton on 4 March 1980. He finished second, and just four days later at a separate event, finished fourth in his first steeplechase at Sandown. Later the same year, Charles rode his own horse, Allibar, into a highly creditable second place in an amateur riders' handicap chase at Ludlow. After being unseated at Sandown in the Grand Military Gold Cup on his own horse, Good Prospect, he rode his sixth and final race at Newton Abbot on 21 May 1981, finishing ninth on Upton Grey, a horse owned by his grandmother, the Queen Mother.

Polo was always Charles's favourite equine sport and he started to play seriously in 1970, when Ronald Ferguson became his polo manager. 'He was a good player,' Ronald Ferguson confirmed. 'He didn't dabble at it. He's a fine horseman, he is strong, and he's got guts. He is dedicated to polo; he'll be devastated when he has to give it up for good.'

The Prince of Wales finally gave up polo in 1992, having suffered many falls, including one two years previously for which he needed lengthy treatment. He now restricts his riding mainly to official duties and led the parade and took the salute for the first time as King in the 2023 Trooping the Colour, on his horse Noble, a gift from the Royal

Canadian Mounted Police. As it was the horse's first Trooping, he was not as passive a mount as a more experienced horse might have been, and it took all the King's considerable skill to keep him still.

The late Queen's horses won all the British Classic races at least once, with the exception of the Epsom Derby. Her greatest win was in 2013, when Estimate and jockey Ryan Moore charged home in front of a roaring crowd to claim a first Ascot Gold Cup win for a reigning monarch in the race's 207-year history.

The only person outside the family to have the late Queen's private phone number was her bloodstock and racing advisor, John Warren. He took over the role from his father-in-law, Lord Carnarvon, who died in 2001 after thirty-two years as Her Majesty's racing advisor. To ensure a seamless transition, Warren is now racing advisor to King Charles and Queen Camilla, and all the racehorses run in their joint names. In October 2022, the late Queen's horse Just Fine crossed the finishing line in first place at Leicester, giving King Charles his first winner as monarch, with a prize of £15,000.

Royal Ascot in 2023 confirmed the King's interest in racing when he attended all five days of the royal meeting as the twelfth monarch to patronise the event since Queen Anne founded it in 1711. Having his first Royal Ascot winner, Desert Hero, in the King George V Stakes – which is named after his great-grandfather – sealed Charles's interest.

'Think how proud our grandmother, the Queen, would've

been,' Zara Tindall said in an interview for television. 'To have a winner for Charles and Camilla and keep that dream alive, was incredible. It's a new excitement.'

As it has done for centuries, the horse will always play an important part in the lives of kings and queens. Perhaps there is a hereditary royal gene passed down through the generations that gives an affinity for the animal. In the immortal words that William Shakespeare put into the mouth of King Richard III at the Battle of Bosworth Field, where he lost his life: 'A horse! A horse! My kingdom for a horse!'

4

My Mother's Sister, Princess Margaret

Brought up in regal isolation, Princess Margaret was always protective of her elder sister and never more so than after Lilibet had given birth to her first child. Her sister had won the man she wanted and had a child within a year of the marriage – a son to secure the succession. Margaret was not so fortunate. Suitors always surrounded her, but none who could match her. She was wilful, contrary and an impossible mixture of tenderness, arrogance and self-entitlement.

Prince Charles adored her. She was one of his godparents and held him as he was baptised in the christening robes she and Lilibet had once worn themselves. After the ceremony, Margaret was heard to say wittily, 'I suppose I'll now be known as Charlie's Aunt.'

This catchy phrase made its way into almost every newspaper and periodical in the Western world, such was Margaret's star appeal. When her godson Charles married Lady Diana Spencer, both women instantly got along.

The only time she really disapproved was in November 1984, when Princess Diana travelled beside the Queen in the carriage to the State Opening of Parliament. Diana had a new hairstyle that day – a badly constructed chignon (her hair was too short for the style and in the early '80s hair extensions were not as professional as they are today). Despite Diana's insistence, her stylist, Kevin Shanley, had refused to do the look, with the excuse that he wasn't good enough, and left it to his assistant, Richard Dalton, to pin a pleat of hair into Diana's own, which had the double advantage of giving some bulk and keeping Diana's tiara in place. The following morning *The Times* published a picture on its front page – not of the Queen but of a smiling, waving Diana with a caption describing her new hairstyle.

'How could you let her, Lilibet?' Princess Margaret berated her sister. 'How could you let her upstage you?' Of all the members of the royal family, Margaret had been the most supportive of Diana and had always stood up for her when her childish outbursts had tested everyone else's patience. She even had a sneaking admiration for the way Diana had struggled to maintain her own identity in the face of the many demands of her newfound station. Margaret had faced a similar situation after Elizabeth became Queen, and in an effort to assert herself, had deliberately worn whatever colour dress her sister was wearing, much to the irritation of Prince Philip, who, red-faced with annoyance, would remind her of her position in the constitutional pecking order.

What Margaret had never done was challenge the Queen

at such a formal and solemn occasion as the State Opening of Parliament, and she was outraged by Diana's action. If Elizabeth was prepared to give Diana the benefit of the doubt, her sister was not. Margaret knew that Diana was making something of a fool out of her husband and believed, like most of the family, that if Charles had been firmer in the beginning, many of the later difficulties would have been avoided. But Charles was either too accommodating, too timid or, as many of the household staff maintained, too weak to call Diana to order. Like his mother and grandmother, Charles hated confrontation and did what he usually did when faced with a crisis beyond his immediate control: turned away from it.

This course of inaction would come to haunt Charles over the years. His youngest son, Prince Harry, complained how difficult it was to get hold of 'Pa', as he calls him, when his father didn't want to take his calls, which he frequently didn't. After Harry and Meghan married, there was seldom a simple phone call from his father. They all contained various demands or requests, sometimes wrapped up in niceties, sometimes not. Again, had Charles been firmer with Harry and, to some extent, William, in their formative years, they might not have caused him so much worry. In Harry's case, this ultimately appears to have manifested in his being unwilling to take responsibility for his own actions and blaming everyone else when things don't work out the way he wants.

Diana was somewhat correct in her belief that Charles's rigorous upbringing had made it difficult for him to communicate emotionally, but she failed to understand the old-fashioned restrictions of the era in which he was born. Aristocratic parents saw little of their children, leaving their upbringing to the care of nannies and governesses. Nanny ruled the nursery and often ruled the mother, who relied on Nanny to ensure the children stuck to a strict routine. Good manners were drilled into children without much thought for their own small feelings. There was very little physical contact with parents; not that they didn't care – it was just not how people were brought up in those days. Feelings were not considered much, conformity and good behaviour were far more important.

'Margo', as she was known, had become very fond of her nephew. As a toddler, Charles was left behind with his grandparents, Margaret and nanny Helen Lightbody when Elizabeth travelled to Malta, where Philip was serving with the Royal Navy. In those days it was considered neither safe nor healthy to travel abroad with young children, and so they were always left behind. On one of those occasions, Margaret wrote to her friend the American heiress Sharman Douglas, reminding her that when they had been at the 400 Club in Leicester Square, Douglas had expressed an interest in meeting little Prince Charles. 'You said you'd like to come and see my heavenly nephew,' Margaret wrote. 'I don't know quite when you stop work but . . . I would adore to show him to you.'

Later, when her sister was even busier, after her accession, Margo would spend time in the schoolroom at Buckingham Palace, where they lived after their all-too-short tenure at

Clarence House. Charles and his governess, Miss Peebles had most of their lessons alone, but sometimes Margaret would slip in to look at what he was doing, ostensibly so she could report back to the Queen, but mainly because she enjoyed it.

When King George VI died, in February 1952, Charles and his sister Anne were far too young to have been considered able to attend their grandfather's funeral and remained at Sandringham. This was not the case with the coronation the following June, and the Queen and Philip decided that Charles, as Duke of Cornwall, should see at least part of the coronation service and be in the care of Princess Margaret when the day came.

After discussing the logistics of getting Charles to the Abbey on 2 June, it fell to Margo and the Queen Mother to supervise him. They decided he should sit between them in the front of the Royal Gallery box so that they could curtail his four-year-old fidgeting. He could then stay for part of the ceremony or as much as they judged he could take, and then Nanny Lightbody would escort him home. On the morning of the coronation, Nanny looked out of the window at the wet, cold June day with dismay as she dressed her small, excited charge in white silk trousers and a shirt with an elaborate lace jabot. She then took him down to a side door of Buckingham Palace, from where they were driven on a circuitous route to Dean's Yard and the Cloisters, and so into Westminster Abbey itself. Nanny saw Charles into the Royal Gallery and waited while he was slipped unnoticed to the front row, between his grandmother and Princess Margaret. According to his official chronicler, Dermot Morrah, he arrived there at the most solemn and sacramental moment of the service:

> The choir was singing Handel's joyous setting of the anthem 'Zadok the Priest', which has stood in the coronation order (at first in the Latin version) without a break since King Edgar the Peaceful was crowned in Bath in 973. The Queen had been stripped of her splendid crimson robes and now, in the plainest possible white garment with no jewels save her earrings, was taking her seat in the coronation chair while four knights of the garter held over a canopy of cloth of gold. It was the moment that she was to be raised to the sanctified rank of queenhood by the anointing with consecrated oil.

Having rubbed his hands over his own head, little Charles held them out to his grandmother to smell the pomade Nanny Lightbody had been given by the palace barber, who had cut his hair. Charles's only recollection is that his hair was plastered 'with the most appalling gunge'. He tugged frequently at his grandmother's sleeve and asked questions of both her and Princess Margaret, but has no memory of what exactly it was that excited his attention. There was so much to ask about and so much time to fidget that they decided that Nanny should take him back to the palace before he became too agitated.

When the coronation party returned to Buckingham Palace, Charles and Anne ran about trying to grab hold of the Queen Mother's huge purple train, while photographer Baron was attempting to get the official photographs done as quickly as possible as the light disappeared outside. The Queen went out onto the balcony to acknowledge the immense roaring chorus of cheers, still wearing her robes and the crown. Prince Philip led the children out to witness the extraordinary scene before the royal party finally came inside.

As she came inside, the Queen at last removed the heavy crown and put it on a table. Lady Glenconner, one of her maids of honour, noticed Prince Charles making 'a beeline for it'. She recalled, 'We thought he was going to drop it. I thought, "Oh, my goodness, that would be a bad omen." But luckily, I think my mother, as a lady-in-waiting, seized it from him and took it away.'

Prince Charles had had plenty of opportunity to take a shine to the giant crown as the future Queen had practised wearing it so she could get used to it. Charles has a memory of her coming to kiss him goodnight wearing it, and Anne Glenconner also recalls her wearing it as she was writing letters. 'I think Prince Charles said he remembers going in and seeing her wearing it, and asked her what she was doing. She explained she was practising, which was sensible as the crown weighed at least five pounds!'

While the rest of the grown-ups sipped champagne, the Queen made her way to the upper floor to visit the party that Charles and Anne were having with some of the children of the royal household staff. As she entered, they squealed with excitement to see her in her regalia. She gave

Charles and Anne a quick kiss and made her way back downstairs, conscious that she would not see much of them again that day.

For Margaret, her sister's coronation provided the moment for the press to discover her secret love for Group Captain Peter Townsend, her late father's former equerry. She famously brushed a piece of fluff off his uniform after the coronation ceremony and was caught doing so by a photographer, who correctly judged it to be newsworthy. What had started as a schoolgirl crush on a married man sixteen years her senior who had two young children was allowed to develop because no one thought anything of it – until the crush became the real thing.

This was the first of many problems faced by the young Queen, who understood that working for the royal family is like a marriage – to the royal family. They simply don't seem to realise that someone might have an outside life, and this was especially the case in the early days of Elizabeth's reign. Townsend had a wife called Rosemary, but she became thoroughly disillusioned with her husband's devotion to the job rather than to her and their young family.

Many years later, staff working for the then Prince of Wales complained of his demands on their time. He would call at any hour, night or day, that the whim took him, and would ask for things to be done immediately, regardless of what anyone was already doing or even if they were on holiday. He explained to me that it was because his memory was so bad, he needed to do things at once or he forgot.

The only person who noticed a difference in Margaret's behaviour when she was around Townsend had been her father, the King. The two were so close that he quickly deduced that something was going on, but the King was not at all well and was fighting what he thought was pneumonitis, so he took no action. It was in fact lung cancer, and it was too late for him to be able to extinguish the flames of the affair. After the death of the King, Margaret leaned on Townsend more than ever. In November 1952, Townsend told the Queen and Prince Philip that he and Margaret were madly in love and wanted to marry, for which he had to have her consent. He had just obtained his divorce from his wife Rosemary and later wrote how impressed he was 'by the Queen's movingly simple and sympathetic acceptance of the disturbing fact of her sister's love for me.'

What Townsend didn't say was how deeply shocked the Queen was about the implications of them wanting to marry. Apart from the constitutional situation, whereby members of the royal family could not marry divorcees in the eyes of the Church at that time, Townsend was divorced, already had children and was much older than her sister, whom he had secretly romanced right under their noses. When the Queen Mother was eventually told, she was equally upset, although she put on a brave front. She discussed it with her elder daughter and wrote to Tommy Lascelles, now the Queen's private secretary. 'I would like to talk to you soon, please,' she wrote. 'I have nobody I can talk to about such dreadful things.' When she finally spoke to him, she wept, which was understandable: her husband was gone, her elder daughter was Queen and her younger daughter looked as if she might bring disrepute to the new reign that they were trying so hard to put in place.

In his autobiography, *Time and Chance*, Townsend eloquently describes the tension and drama that led up to the end of the affair. The press was on the side of the lovers but complained that after two years since their relationship became public, they should make up their minds. The Queen was portrayed as being on the side of the Church, as its Supreme Governor, and the establishment figures of the day, which included members of the Privy Council, were described as antagonistic and unhelpful. They could not prevent the marriage, but they could influence Parliament, to whom the veto, when relinquished by the Sovereign, then passed. 'She would have nothing left – except me,' Townsend wrote. 'It was too much to ask of her, too much for her to give. We should be left with nothing, but our devotion to face the world.'

The whole affair came to a head in October 1955. 'We felt mute and numbed at the centre of this maelstrom,' Townsend wrote, recalling the time Princess Margaret drove to Windsor Castle to join her mother, the Queen and the Duke of Edinburgh for lunch. Exactly what was said or happened that day has never been disclosed, but facing up to the gravity of the state of affairs, they discussed the Princess's situation together.

Later that day, Margaret rang Townsend 'in great distress'. She did not say what had passed between her and her sister and brother-in-law, 'but doubtless the stern truth was dawning on her,' he observed.

Prince Philip decided to keep his silence during the discussions, but he was there to lend a private ear to the Queen when she needed his support, which of course she did. As Queen, she was just too close and emotionally involved to decide between her wish for her sister's happiness and the need for the royal family to do the right thing.

On Monday 31 October 1955, Margaret and Townsend met for the last time. Their love story ended with words crafted by Townsend on a rough piece of paper. This became the Princess's statement later broadcast to the world. When she read out what Townsend had written, she quietly and sadly agreed: 'I have decided not to marry Group Captain Townsend,' she began when the statement was issued that evening at 7 p.m., and continued, 'I have reached this decision entirely alone, and in doing so I have been strengthened by the unfailing support and devotion of Group Captain Townsend.'

And so, Margaret relinquished her love for the sake of royal duty. The role the young Queen was obliged to play in the destruction of her sister's first passionate love affair was stressful and affected her deeply. She blamed herself for Margaret's unhappiness and tried to cheer her up, but Margaret remained tense. Many years later, when Charles ascended the throne as King, he too had family problems that affected public opinion and directly swayed his subjects' view of the monarchy. One of them was deciding how to help the Duke of York, and the other was the ongoing problem of the Duke and Duchess of Sussex. Charles had only been King for four months when Harry's book denigrating the institution of the monarchy appeared on the shelves, followed by several interviews that revealed just what he thought of the institution and the royal family, which, like it or not, Harry is still a part of.

Four years after her statement, Prince Philip walked Princess Margaret down the aisle on her wedding day. It was the first royal wedding to be fully televised, and the Duke of Edinburgh accompanied Margaret from Buckingham Palace to Westminster Abbey in the Glass Coach. Her husband-to-be, Antony Armstrong-Jones, couldn't have been more different from Peter Townsend, but he appeared to make Margaret happy and the Queen was pleased her sister had found what she thought was a more suitable kind of love. She remained the Queen's adored sister and was very much a royal princess – but she never let anyone forget it if they did not treat her with due respect. As a young woman, she had always felt that the Queen was so good and perfect, while she was very much the opposite, doomed to an unhappy marriage and a succession of unsuitable romances. Later she found a new kind of confidence and, for the first time in her life, she felt able to give the Queen advice, rather than the other way around. The ironic poignancy of this reversal of their situations was not lost on the Queen or Prince Philip. This was not how anyone could ever have seen things turning out, with Margaret at ease with herself and her children happily settled, while the Queen and Philip were faced with three out of their four children getting divorced.

Princess Margaret prided herself on being a good mother and it made her feel that at least she had managed to get something right. Unlike her sister, who put her husband before the children, Princess Margaret put her children first. For all her personal problems and temperamental behaviour, she was a natural mother. Even though she had a wonderful nanny, Nanny Sumner, if one of her children, David and Sarah, cried in the night it was Margaret who climbed out of bed to comfort them. She breastfed both babies and even changed their nappies between official engagements. When her children were grown up, she became an indulgent mother but gracefully let them both go from her life, which was quite a sacrifice. She was often lonely but she did not cling to them, and as a result they always took the trouble to drop in and see her because they wanted to, not because they felt obliged. They were both favourites of the Queen and always spent time with her at Balmoral in the summer and at Sandringham for Christmas.

Lady Sarah Chatto, who is married to the artist and actor Daniel Chatto, was staying at Balmoral for a shooting weekend with her husband when the Queen was taken ill. Frail, but in the best of spirits, the Queen hosted a dinner party for her guests in the Balmoral dining room on the Sunday night. The only unusual thing guests noticed was that the Queen's eyes were unusually bloodshot, and instead of dressing for dinner in black tie as is usual at Balmoral, they were all told to dress casually. As the outgoing prime minister Boris Johnson was due to arrive in two days' time, followed by the incoming prime minister Liz Truss, all the guests made themselves scarce the following day to enable Her Majesty to have some peace. Three days later, the Queen died.

Lady Sarah has always been very fond of her cousin Charles, and vice versa, so she was among the first to offer her sincere and heartfelt condolences to the new King. He took an interest in helping her with her painting at Balmoral and Sandringham during the holidays; they even went painting together in Italy. As much as she cared for the Prince, Sarah later admitted being stunned by the way his valet, Michael Fawcett, fussed and fawned around him, and couldn't believe that anyone could bear to have their every whim catered for, as Fawcett did for Charles. She said she thought it was bad for anyone to be indulged in such a way, thus making Charles too dependent on people around him instead of getting on with it himself.

Sarah had seen her own mother cosseted by royal staff but she had come from an older generation who took it for granted, and it was never anything like Fawcett and Charles. She confessed she thought it would be a good thing for Charles to lose someone like Fawcett. She was eventually proven right when, in 2022, Fawcett was involved in a 'cash for honours' scandal following claims that he had tried to secure a knighthood and British citizenship for a Saudi tycoon who had donated more than £1.5 million to the Prince's charities. This made Fawcett's position untenable and led to him having to resign his position as chief executive of the Prince's Foundation. It was a bitter blow to Charles, as not only was Fawcett brilliant at schmoozing the right people, in addition his organising abilities were second to none. He also had an artistic eye and could turn a dinner table into something quite magnificent in the minimum of time.

A lot of people who work for the royal family have, in a sense, given up their lives to do so. They then substitute their lives for the royals' lives and live through them. Because Michael Fawcett didn't have his own interests outside his job (until he started his company with his wife, Debbie, who was a former royal housemaid), he fell in love with his royal job and all that went with it. It is the fate of many staff who have worked for the royal family for most of their formative years and something the Queen was very attuned to. She would look after them as if they were her children, paying personally for any extra medical care or therapy and listening to their tales of woe about broken love affairs.

The love affairs she never got a chance to mend were those of her sister Margo and son Charles. Both of them had suffered a great deal from their unhappy marriages and the Queen had been unable to help. Prince Philip thought she should have tackled the Diana-and-Charles problem sooner and reminded them of their duty and commitments years beforehand. They might then have been able to salvage what was left of their relationship. Instead, the Queen did what she often did, which was hope things would get better in time. Prince Philip called it 'sitting on the fence'. He also thought that the Townsend affair should have been dealt with differently, that instead of giving the couple hope they could eventually marry and then expecting them to wait for two years, a decision should have been made much sooner so they could have repaired their lives.

Prince Philip had tried to talk to Prince Charles about his marital difficulties and the effect they were having on the institution he was born to head. It was meant as fatherly advice, but because of the distant nature of their relationship, the two found it uncomfortable to exchange confidences and their conversations usually ended with Charles looking at his watch and making an excuse to leave the room. Thwarted in his own efforts to introduce some sense into an increasingly senseless situation, Philip asked his wife to bring her considerable authority to bear. The Queen consistently refused to do this, much to Philip's exasperation. Often so intimidating to those outside her own family who overstepped the mark, the Queen was unwilling to confront those within it.

Margaret had no sympathy left for the Princess of Wales, despite the similarity of their predicaments. Once so supportive of the Princess, she became as vocal as Prince Philip in her condemnation. She felt Diana had let the Queen down, as had her nephew, Prince Charles. As far as she was concerned, it was an impossible situation as there was little she could do except listen to her sister and offer her the comfort she could.

One person within the family who was full of sympathy for Prince Charles's unhappy marriage was his second cousin, Princess Alexandra, nicknamed 'Pud' by the royal family. She and her husband, Angus Ogilvy, had a difficult time in 1989 when their daughter Marina, Charles's goddaughter, discovered she was pregnant by a man her parents did not approve of at all – when Marina met free-lance photographer Paul Mowatt, she threw away her hard-won place at the Guildhall School of Music to go and live with him.

Marina's parents were furious when confronted with the news of their unwed daughter's pregnancy. Their disappointment in their talented daughter was heightened by the worry of what effect Marina's behaviour would have on the royal family. According to Marina, her mother told her to have an abortion or get married straight away. Instead, Marina sold her story to the *Today* newspaper for a rumoured £250,000, which was a huge amount of money in 1989. The situation quickly got out of hand and Marina made several hysterical accusations, including that she had been cut off by her parents and thrown out of her home. Then she wrote a letter to the Queen asking for advice and support. When Marina revealed what she had done, it made even more embarrassing headlines, especially as she admitted that she had delivered the six-page letter to 'Dear Cousin Lilibet' by hand to Buckingham Palace and the Queen had not replied.

It was a painful situation for everyone, especially when Marina appeared on television to beg her parents to get in touch with her. The scandal was spiralling out of control, with Marina continuing to act as if she were under some sort of compulsion to distress her parents and the royal family in any way possible. 'This,' said Marina boldly, 'is the dark side of the royal family we are experiencing now. The other side of the postcard is just for tourists.'

Her defiance has echoes of the Duke and Duchess of Sussex some thirty years later – their television interviews, their documentaries and Harry's autobiography, all with one central theme: a public gripe against members of the royal family. It is not surprising the Queen remained outwardly unmoved when dealing with scandal from within her family, as there was nothing she hadn't seen before.

Marina and Paul Mowatt eventually got married and the pregnant bride wore black. The Queen made no secret of her displeasure. Traditionally, Her Majesty would have given her consent to a marriage within the family with a handwritten, vellum document addressed, in this case, to 'My trusty and well-beloved cousin'. This written permission from the monarch is necessary before any churchman can perform the wedding ceremony. For more than 200 years, every bride and groom from the royal family has been given this document and so indeed was Marina – but with a difference.

After calling a special meeting of the Privy Council to authorise the wedding (she was obliged to do so under the rules of the Royal Marriages Act of 1772), the Queen gave her consent. Buckingham Palace, however, when sending the vellum to the Crown Office in the Lord Chancellor's department for the final inscription, gave instructions that the words 'My trusty and well-beloved cousin' should be deleted.

The Queen was all about forgiveness but she did not forget. Several years later, Lady Elizabeth Anson was going through the Queen's Christmas card list with her when they came to Marina's name. 'I think not,' the Queen said, and she put a pencil line through it.

5

POWERFUL INFLUENCES

Of the late Queen's relations, there were two whose lives had an enormous impact on both her and Prince Charles, namely her uncle the Duke of Windsor and Earl Mountbatten of Burma.

If the uncrowned King Edward VIII had not signed the instrument of abdication, Princess Elizabeth's father, the Duke of York, would never have become monarch and the Princess would not have inherited the throne except in the unlikely event that her uncle, once king, had remained childless. But Edward was a man used to getting his own way, and when he was forced to choose between continuing as King or marrying the twice-divorced Wallis Simpson, he decided he would rather renounce the throne than live without her. Thus, the course of history was changed.

'I do hereby declare my irrevocable determination to renounce the throne for myself and for my descendants, and my desire that effect should be given to this instrument of abdication immediately.' With these words, and after a reign of less than one year, King Edward VIII signed the instrument of abdication on 10 December 1936 in the presence of his brothers Princes Albert, Henry and George at Fort Belvedere at Windsor, which as Prince of Wales he had made his home since 1929.

The following day, Edward spoke to the nation from Windsor Castle in a speech transmitted on BBC Radio:

> You all know the reasons which have impelled me to renounce the throne. But I want you to understand that in making up my mind I did not forget the country or the Empire, which, as Prince of Wales, and lately as King, I have for twenty-five years tried to serve. But you must believe me when I tell you that I have found it impossible to carry the heavy burden of responsibility and to discharge my duties as King as I would wish to do without the help and support of the woman I love.

According to the late historical biographer Lady Longford, the then prime minister Winston Churchill had vetted and improved the abdication speech, adding the phrase about 'the woman I love' that, as Longford put it, 'made a great impression'. The general feeling among the establishment, in the words of Bernard Fitzalan-Howard, 16th Duke of Norfolk, who was Earl Marshal at the time, 'was that Mrs Simpson was so ambitious and she got hold of Edward VIII and really dominated him. And the royal family were not very proud of this. They loathed her and the Queen Mother absolutely hated her. And they never made her into "Her Royal Highness" – she was Duchess; it was not Her Royal Highness.'

The two Princesses, Elizabeth and Margaret, first became aware of what was happening when they heard the cheering of the crowds as their father was proclaimed King on 11 December, following a meeting of the Accession Council. The two girls were in the house on Hyde Park Corner; Princess Elizabeth ran downstairs and a footman told her that her father was King. She came back up and relayed the news to her little sister, who was six at the time. Princess Margaret reportedly asked whether that meant Elizabeth would become Queen. Elizabeth responded, 'Yes, someday,' to which Princess Margaret said, 'Poor you.'

'She must have been very much aware of the burden of her father assuming the monarchy when he did, because he was a sensitive man,' said Sir Gordon Jewkes, former Governor of the Falkland Islands. Royal biographer Philip Ziegler claimed that 'by the end of 1936 when he [the King] found himself popped on the throne, Princess Elizabeth was ten years old and so those enormously important formative years had been spent as a kind of informal family.'

Some twenty years later, Edward Duke of Windsor, on one of his rare visits to England from his home in France, returned to Windsor Castle. He found the room in which he had made his abdication broadcast unchanged, with the furniture covered in dustsheets. Reflecting on that historic occasion, he wrote in his memoir, entitled *A Family Album*, 'I found I had no twinge of regret, leading, as the Duchess and I have since done, a very happy and contented private life'.

Edward's life falls into two parts. As the heir to the throne, he was created the Prince of Wales on his sixteenth birthday. He was handsome, sporting and very popular with people. He toured the British Empire tirelessly and was received with enthusiastic crowds wherever he went. But after his abdication, he became reviled by his family, was seen as a Nazi sympathiser and was banished from the United Kingdom to live abroad for the rest of his life.

Although Edward had been to the Royal Naval College at Osborne, on the Isle of Wight, and had served for a few months in the Royal Navy as a midshipman aboard the battleship HMS *Hindustan*, when war broke out in 1914 he joined the Grenadier Guards and was posted to France. He made many visits to the front line on the Western Front, which were not without risk, and was awarded the Military Cross, all of which made him a well-liked figure with servicemen.

After the war, Edward undertook a series of world tours visiting large parts of what was then the British Empire. Everywhere he travelled he was met with vast crowds wanting to shake his hand, and on a visit to Cape Town in 1922, his right wrist became so swollen from shaking hands that he had to use his left hand. It was on one of these extended cruises in a British warship that he engaged the services of his cousin Lord Louis Mountbatten as equerry; they would remain on friendly terms for the rest of Edward's life.

The many functions in the different countries that Edward attended necessitated frequent changes of uniform. He travelled with forty large trunks of clothing to accommodate all these changes, each trunk numbered and with its contents listed in a series of inventory notebooks. Edward's valet Jack Crisp would organise all the items needed three days in advance, together with any medals and decorations to be worn. Edward's father, King George V, was a stickler for correct attire and would scrutinise the press photographs of his sons' tours for any detail of dress that he considered wrong. If he found anything amiss he would follow up with a correction and reprimand.

During this period Edward began to develop a less formal approach to the traditionally correct clothing to be worn for formal events and adopted a more casual style in his own outfits, to his father's intense annoyance. With his film-star looks he became the most photographed celebrity of his time and every detail of his attire was reported on by the press. During his 1924 visit to the United States, the magazine *Men's Wear Review* reported that the 'average young man in America is more interested in the clothes of the Prince of Wales than in any other individual on earth'. An interest in changing fashion became a lifelong passion for Edward. Among other novelties, he popularised plus fours for golf, turn-ups for trousers and jodhpurs for riding. In the style of his grandfather, Edward VII, who was the first to wear a formal jacket without tails for the evening, he popularised the dinner jacket and owned one in dark navy with black silk-trimmed lapels – very unusual in those days.

When at home in England, Edward enjoyed party-going and London nightlife. He frequented nightclubs such as the Embassy Club, Quaglino's and the Café de Paris, where he regularly danced the night away. One of his diary entries at the time reads: 'My dancing is improving, I got in at 4 a.m.' He was so renowned for his dancing that a popular song of the time contained the lyric 'I danced with a man who danced with a girl who danced with the Prince of Wales.' George V continued to criticise him for his dress and his lifestyle. He once wrote to Edward: 'I hear you were seen at a ball last night where you were not wearing gloves. Do not let this happen again.'

In 1929, the King gave Fort Belvedere, a recently vacated property on the Crown Estate, to his son to use as a country residence. This was where Edward entertained his friends in a relaxed atmosphere, far away from the formality of court, which he increasingly disliked. He had affairs with numerous women, two of whom were married ladies. This infuriated his father, who began to worry about Edward's suitability to inherit the crown. 'After I am dead the boy will ruin himself in twelve months,' he said. The King favoured his second son Bertie and had become inordinately fond of Bertie's wife, Elizabeth Duchess of York. She was the only person who could get away with breaking

Five-month-old Prince Charles takes the proceedings seriously as he and his smiling mother, Princess Elizabeth, pose for their first informal photographs in Buckingham Palace in April 1949.

King George VI and his grandson were photographed at Buckingham Palace to celebrate the toddler's third birthday in November 1951. It was the first photograph of the King after his lung operation the previous September and one of Princess Elizabeth's favourites.

Aged nine months, Prince Charles makes a grab for his grandfather King George VI's stick as his nurse, Helen Lightbody, carries him from Ballater station on the way to Balmoral Castle in August 1949. On the left, Princess Elizabeth stands next to Canon W. E. Adams (far left), provost of Ballater.

The women he loved: the Queen Mother, Prince Charles and Princess Margaret in June 1951, returning to Buckingham Palace following Trooping the Colour. Princess Elizabeth took the salute at the ceremony on behalf of her father the King, who was ill.

The Queen with Princess Anne, who was just five, and Prince Charles, who was almost seven, with nurse Helen Lightbody in August 1955. They are supporting a loca Highland sale to help raise funds for the building of a new vestry at Crathie Kirk.

Prince Charles aged two with his young nurse Mabel Anderson, watching a procession from the gardens of Clarence House.

Prince Charles's beloved governess Miss Peebles, known as 'Mispy', walks with him and Princess Anne through Green Park in November 1954. They had been to see their grandmother, the Queen Mother, at Clarence House.

A rare photograph of the young Prince Charles in 1955. The Queen's press secretary had just instructed newspaper editors to allow the Prince to go on educational visits around London, such as to Madame Tussaud's, without being followed by photographers.

Queen Elizabeth II, who had just celebrated her thirty-fifth birthday, enjoying riding with her son Prince Charles at Windsor Castle in the spring of 1961. Their love of horses was something they always had in common.

Still riding at the age of ninety-four, the Queen is pictured on her fell pony Balmoral Fern in Windsor Home Park in May 2020. Horses were the Queen's lifelong love and she had an incredible knowledge of breeding and bloodlines.

On 26 July 1958, the Queen announced that Prince Charles was to be created the Prince of Wales, although he was not invested until 1969. This photograph shows the Prince wearing his new school uniform for Cheam preparatory school, which he attended from the age of eight.

the King's rigid rules of punctuality for meals. On one occasion she arrived a few minutes late for lunch. She tried to apologise profusely but the King brushed aside her apology, insisting that she was not late and that he had sat down to the meal a minute or two early.

It was Mrs Freda Ward, one of Edward's married mistresses, who introduced him in 1930 to the American divorcee Wallis Simpson, who was at that time married to her second husband, Ernest. Edward became obsessed with Wallis and within a short time she was constantly at his side. His infatuation with her was such that there was nothing he would not do for her. A guest at the Fort reported seeing Edward ask Wallis to light a cigarette for him. 'Only if you ask properly,' she said, whereupon Edward got down on his knees and appeared to beg like a dog.

When he was with Wallis, Edward began to overlook his duties as Prince of Wales. Confidential government papers were left lying around at the Fort for any guest to read, and documents requiring Edward's signature were sometimes returned bearing wine stains. The King and Queen Mary refused to receive Wallis at Buckingham Palace as she was a divorcee. At the time, divorce was considered a disgrace and contrary to the laws of the Church of England, of which the King was the head. Divorced persons were not, for example, permitted to enter the Royal Enclosure at the annual meeting at Ascot racecourse in June.

It was only in December 1936, after Edward had

announced his abdication, that the British people were made aware of the existence of Mrs Simpson. The British press had been silent on the subject even though the American papers and magazines had been keeping up a running commentary on the relationship for months.

In the early hours of 12 December 1936, Edward left England for France. He married Wallis six months later on 3 June 1937. The whole of the royal family boycotted the wedding and Edward fell out with his brother, who issued letters patent that denied Wallis the style of 'Her Royal Highness'. Edward also demanded an exorbitant amount of money to sell back to the King the royal residences and estates of Sandringham and Balmoral he had inherited, which in normal circumstances would have passed to the monarch.

Against the advice of the British government, Edward and Wallis accepted an invitation to visit Germany in October 1937, where they met with Adolf Hitler at his mountain retreat, the Berchtesgaden. They were then photographed giving the Nazi salute and were entertained by Goebbels and Göring. This visit caused further difficulties for Edward's relationship with the royal family and the King threatened to cut off Edward's financial allowance if he returned to Britain.

Things became so bad that Edward wrote to his mother Queen Mary in 1939 saying, 'Your last letter destroyed the last vestige of feeling I had left for you and has made further correspondence between us impossible.'

Just over thirty years later, at the beginning of February 1972, the Duke, who was in poor health, hosted his old friend Dickie Mountbatten at his Paris home and they talked late into the night. As Mountbatten was leaving, the Duke had paused and said: 'There's something I'll bet you don't realise. If I hadn't abdicated, I'd have completed thirty-six years of my reign by now – longer than either my father or grandfather.'

Understandably, the Duke of Windsor was prone to thinking about what might have become of his life, especially when he met with his niece the Queen during her state visit to Paris in 1972 with Prince Philip and Prince Charles. On 18 May, the group arrived at the house in the Bois de Boulogne for tea with the ailing Duke – he had been diagnosed with throat cancer the previous year and was so weak with illness that he had to be given a blood transfusion via a concealed intravenous drip, so the visit only lasted half an hour.

Nurses cared for him on a round-the-clock basis and he must have known his end was not far off, but he insisted to the last that he had no regrets about Wallis, as he confirmed to his friend David Bruce: 'I've spent the best part of my life with her and I can tell you that nothing I gave up for her equals what she has given me: happiness of course, but also meaning. I have found her to be utterly without faults, the perfect woman.'

Wallis may have been the perfect woman, but despite the fact that her bedroom was on the same floor as the Duke's and separated only by a large sitting room, she never visited him in these final days, according to night nurse Julie Chatard Alexander: 'She never came to see him or kiss him good night or see how he was. Not once.'

The Duke was not alone, as his loyal butler Sydney Johnson always looked after him alongside the nursing staff. Johnson had been with the couple since he was sixteen when he started working for them during their time in the Bahamas in the early 1940s.

'On the day he died,' Johnson told me during a visit to the house in the Bois de Boulogne in 1987 for an article in *Majesty* magazine,

he asked me to take him to his desk so he could write some letters. I got him up and sat him at his desk, but he couldn't hold his pen as he was shaking too much. I suggested he had something to eat – perhaps his favourite Finnan haddock and scrambled eggs – but he insisted it wasn't food he needed. 'They're feeding me through my veins, Sydney. All that is behind me now and I don't want anything. I don't feel like anything except maybe some peaches and cream.'

I ran downstairs to the kitchen and got some fresh peaches and cream and put it in front of him. He started putting the spoon to his mouth, but he was trembling so much he couldn't eat. So, I fed him and he drank all the cream. Then he felt tired and wanted to go back to bed, so I sponged him down as I always did and put him to bed with the curtains drawn. It was the last time I saw him alive.

At about two or three o'clock in the afternoon, Johnson went back into the bedroom to see the Duke, who was still sleeping. When he alerted her to this, the Duchess told Johnson not to worry, but he knew she was concerned as he heard her mumbling, 'This is a bad sign.'

That night, of 28 May 1972, he died. 'The Duchess was not with him,' Johnson remembered, 'but I could hear her crying. I went to ask her if I could do something. "Do what you want, Sydney," she said. "They're coming from London to embalm him. Don't interfere. Just brush his hair the way he does it and then leave him. They know what they are doing."'

When the embalmers arrived in Paris, Johnson insisted on dressing the Duke in one of his favourite nightshirts, which Johnson had sewn himself, and put a dressing gown around his emaciated form. It was the last thing he was ever to do for the Duke.

On 31 May, the Duke's body was flown to RAF Benson and was met by a royal guard of honour, his widow and the Duke and Duchess of Kent. The oak coffin lay overnight in the RAF chapel and was then taken to St George's Chapel at Windsor Castle, where it lay in state for two days. On the last evening Prince Charles and his uncle Dickie Mountbatten took Wallis to see her husband, and she stood with her head bowed in grief. 'He was my entire life,' she said. 'I can't begin to think what I am going to do without him; he gave up so much for me and now he has gone.' It was their thirty-fifth wedding anniversary.

On 5 June 1972, the funeral took place in St George's Chapel, led by the Queen and Prince Philip. Wallis wore a simple Givenchy black dress and coat. After the service there was a lunch for forty people in the state dining room. Wallis sat next to Lord Mountbatten and the Duke of Edinburgh and later recalled her experience of the Duke that day to her friend Aline Griffith, Countess of Romanones: 'I had always imagined he would be better, kinder, perhaps more human than the others, but you know, Aline, he is just a four-flusher [a slang word for a bluffer, derived from the game of poker]. Nor he, or anyone else, offered any solicitude or sympathy whatsoever.' Wallis was exaggerating somewhat, as the Queen had shown her immense sympathy, as had Prince Charles, both knowing that she was in the early stages of dementia. During the funeral service, the Queen had helped her find her place in the order of service and taken great care of her. Even the Queen Mother was understanding, shocked at how old and shrunken Wallis appeared to be.

After lunch, the party moved to the royal burial ground at Frogmore, to a spot the Duke had chosen, near where he had played as a boy. Part of him was still that boy who never grew up, but he made sure before his death that Wallis would be buried next to him. Fourteen years later, in April 1986, she was interred beside her husband, closing a dramatic episode in royal history that continues to fascinate to this day.

The Duke of Windsor was never reconciled with the royal family. Dickie Mountbatten had tried to use his influence on Prince Charles to have an invitation extended to the Duke and Duchess to visit Britain. Charles was receptive to the idea and in March 1970 wrote: 'I personally feel it would be wonderful if Uncle David [Edward, Duke of Windsor] and his wife could come over and spend a weekend. Now that he is getting old, he must long to come back and it would seem pointless to continue the feud.' Charles raised the matter with his grandmother Queen Elizabeth. She was adamant that there should be no such invitation. She blamed Wallis and Edward for bringing her husband George VI to an early death from the stress of taking on the role of King, for which he was unsuited and unprepared. There was no love lost between Wallis and the Queen Mother, whom Wallis described as the 'fat Scotch cook' responsible for her and her husband's exile, while the Queen Mother declared that Wallis was hated by the country at large.

In 1971, the British Ambassador to France, Sir Christopher Soames, had arranged for Prince Charles, who was on a private trip to Paris, to visit the Duke and Duchess of Windsor at their house in the Bois de Boulogne. In his diary Prince Charles describes arriving at the Duke's residence to find a party full of the 'most dreadful American guests I have ever seen', noting that 'most of them were thoroughly tight'. He wrote that he had looked forward to the meeting 'with no small degree of anticipation' but was disappointed to find 'footmen and pages wearing identical uniforms to the ones ours wear at home. It was rather pathetic seeing that.' His uncle David talked about how difficult the royal family had made it for him for the past thirty-five years, and Charles recorded that the 'whole thing seemed so tragic – the existence, the people and the atmosphere – that I was relieved to escape it after 45 minutes.'

After the Duke of Windsor died, Prince Charles corresponded with the Duchess quite a few times. She also came to stay at Windsor Castle on the anniversary of her husband's death so she could visit his grave at Frogmore, and she would sleep in the Shelter Rooms. Usually, one member of the family would be there, often the Duke of Kent, one of the Queen's paternal cousins. The family did try to keep in touch with the Duchess more than they have been given credit for, but it was Maître Suzanne Blum, Wallis's lawyer, who prevented it. It was reported at one point that the Duchess did think of leaving everything to Prince Charles in her will, but again it was the lawyer who persuaded her not to.

The man who Charles always claimed as his mentor was Lord Louis Francis Albert Victor Nicholas Mountbatten, Earl Mountbatten of Burma, born on 25 June 1900 at Frogmore House in Windsor. As the second son of Prince Louis of Battenberg and Princess Victoria of Hesse and by Rhine, and as the great-grandson of Queen Victoria, Lord Mountbatten was uncle to Prince Philip – his sister Princess Alice of Greece being Philip's mother – and a second cousin of Queen Elizabeth II. He was known to the family as 'Dickie', short for his Christian name Nicholas; so many of the Russian Tsar's family, of which Dickie was a member, were named Nicholas shortened to 'Nicky' that it was felt he needed an alternative.

Although born a German, Dickie's father joined the British Royal Navy when he was fourteen years old. After a distinguished naval career, in 1912 he was appointed First Sea Lord, the head of the Royal Navy. When war broke out with Germany, there was a wave of anti-German feeling in Britain; even dachshunds were kicked in the street. In October 1914, Prince Louis – who spoke with a heavy German accent – feeling that the criticisms of him as a German at the head of the Navy were a distraction from the war effort, resigned as First Sea Lord after forty-seven years of naval service. Dickie was devastated – another cadet recalled seeing him with tears running down his cheeks. From that day on, he determined to avenge his father's forced resignation by becoming First Sea Lord himself.

In 1917, King George V decided to drop the Germanic royal name Saxe-Coburg-Gotha and adopt Windsor instead. At the same time, Battenberg was anglicised to Mountbatten and Lord Louis was created 1st Marquess of Milford Haven.

Dickie's father had no great family fortune and, as a professional Navy man, Dickie had no prospect of making a fortune of his own. He solved this problem by marrying Edwina Ashley, a society beauty and heiress to one of the greatest fortunes in the country. Her maternal grandfather was the banker Sir Ernest Cassel, one of the richest men in the world and financial advisor to Edward VII, who was Edwina's godfather and after whom she had been named.

Dickie and Edwina married on 18 July 1922 in what was undoubtedly the wedding of the year. In spite of the rain, 8,000 people had gathered outside St Margaret's, the twelfth-century church behind Westminster Abbey where they were to be married. King George V and Queen Mary, and most members of the royal family, were in attendance, with Prince Edward as best man.

Dickie was a close personal friend of several members of the royal family, including King George VI and Queen Elizabeth. He was a frequent guest at Balmoral and at Windsor Castle. A key figure in the extended family, he was always present on important occasions and could be seen joining the royals on the balcony at Buckingham Palace. Something of an *éminence grise*, he was the mentor of his nephew Prince Philip and became the closest confidant of, and advisor to, Prince Charles. He was also a brilliant strategist and extremely ambitious. Over a period of years, he masterminded a plot to marry a Mountbatten into the British royal family, and Prince Philip was to be part of that plan.

From the age of eight, when Prince Philip was sent to school in England, it was Dickie's mother's family who became the main influences in Philip's life. Initially it was his uncle, George Milford Haven, who acted *in loco parentis*, until he died at the age of forty-five in 1938, when Philip was seventeen. It was then that Dickie took over as Philip's mentor and guide. Philip's father, Prince Andrew of Greece, had written to Dickie: 'I do beg you take charge of Philip's upbringing.' It was Dickie who persuaded Philip to go to Dartmouth naval college rather than joining the Royal Air Force, which was Philip's first choice. Philip had always been keen on flying and in later life became an experienced pilot of many types of aircraft. It was at Dartmouth that Philip had his first significant meeting with Princess Elizabeth.

In 1939, not long after Philip entered the naval college, King George VI and Queen Elizabeth paid a visit, having earlier that day inspected the fleet at Weymouth. On 22 July, the Royal Yacht *Victoria and Albert* anchored in the mouth of the River Dart. On board with the King and Queen were their two daughters, the Princesses Elizabeth and Margaret; also in attendance, in his capacity as aide-de-camp to the King, was Dickie Mountbatten. It was on this occasion that Philip first publicly and knowingly met his future bride, although they had both been present at several royal occasions. When Philip was thirteen and the Princess was eight, they both attended the 1934 wedding of Philip's cousin Princess Marina, later Duchess of Kent, and Elizabeth's uncle Prince George, Duke of Kent. They were also both guests at the coronation of George VI in 1937.

The Princesses' visit was somewhat curtailed due to an outbreak of chicken pox and mumps among the cadets. Elizabeth and Margaret were restricted to the house of the officer in charge of the college, Admiral Sir Frederick Dalrymple-Hamilton. Dickie Mountbatten suggested that of all the cadets, Philip should be given the unenviable job of entertaining the two young girls while the King and

Queen carried out their formal inspection of the college. Not only were Philip and the Princesses distant cousins, but Philip was well known as a friend of the royal family through his mother Princess Alice.

It is clear that Elizabeth fell for Philip at once during that meeting at Dartmouth. In his official biography of King George VI, Sir John Wheeler-Bennett, writes of Philip: 'This was the man with whom Princess Elizabeth had been in love from their first meeting.' Later, when Elizabeth had acceded to the throne, she read the proofs of her father's biography prior to publication and changed not one word of this statement.

After Dartmouth, Philip was initially posted as a midshipman to a battleship in Ceylon, but he wanted to see action and got Dickie to arrange for him to be posted to HMS *Ramillies* in the Mediterranean, whose captain was Vice Admiral Baillie-Grohman. Grohman kept a diary (which is now stored with his papers at Greenwich) that records an interview with his new midshipman, who tells him that Dickie has ideas for his future and thinks he could marry Princess Elizabeth. According to Baillie-Grohman, Philip was already writing to her once a week.

We can only surmise that Elizabeth instigated the correspondence by writing to Philip to thank him for looking after her and her sister at Dartmouth – something any well-brought-up girl would do. It seems that this correspondence went on throughout the war. Philip's cousin Princess Alexandra, in her biography of Philip, recounts meeting him when he was on shore leave in Cape Town in 1941. She says Philip was busy writing a letter. When she asked, 'Who to?' Philip replied, 'Lilibet – Princess Elizabeth of England.'

The MP and renowned diarist Sir Henry 'Chips' Channon found himself in Greece in 1941 at the same time that Philip was enjoying some shore leave in Athens. A diary entry from 21 January refers to 'an enjoyable Greek cocktail party. Prince Philip of Greece was there. He is extraordinarily handsome . . . He is to be our Prince Consort and that is why he is serving in our navy.'

Closer to the end of the war, Dickie recorded in an August 1944 diary entry that he met George VI at the British Embassy in Cairo. He also met with Philip, whose ship was at Alexandria. Dickie claims he had very satisfactory discussions with the King about Philip and Elizabeth.

At some point during the war, Philip and Princess Elizabeth exchanged photographs. Philip kept hers in a leather photo frame in his cabin and she kept his on her dressing table. It was well known among the crew that letters to and from the Princess came through the mailrooms of Philip's ships with regularity.

Philip had seen all four of his sisters marry German noblemen with landed estates and fully staffed palatial homes. He would have been very aware that he could not expect to inherit anything from his father other than a few personal effects. Meanwhile, Princess Elizabeth would one day be one of the richest women in the world. Few young men would not have had their heads turned by the prospect of marrying a beautiful young heiress who would one day be a Queen. The fact that she had fallen deeply in love with Philip at first sight was something that even Dickie could not have foreseen.

Philip felt that Dickie was being overzealous in promoting the engagement and asked him to back off. According to Mountbatten's biographer Philip Ziegler, Philip wrote to Dickie,

> Please, I beg of you not too much advice in an affair of the heart or I shall be forced to do the wooing by proxy . . . I am not being rude but it is apparent that you like the idea of being General Manager of this little show, and I am rather afraid that she [Princess Elizabeth] might not take to the idea quite as docilely as I do. It is true I know what is good for me, but don't forget she has not had you as uncle loco parentis, counsellor, and friend as long as I have.

After the war, in the summer of 1946, Philip was invited to stay with the royal family at Balmoral, where days were spent deer stalking and shooting grouse. It was here that at some point Philip's proposal of marriage was accepted by Elizabeth and approved by her father, the King.

Dickie left English shores to become the last Viceroy of India in 1947. He was able to leave content in the knowledge that his long-term plan had come to fruition. Not only was his nephew about to become officially engaged to Princess Elizabeth, but the name Mountbatten would now be linked to the British crown.

In 1949, two years after his and Elizabeth's celebrated wedding in Westminster Abbey, Philip returned to active naval service as second-in-command of HMS *Chequers* and leader of the First Destroyer Flotilla of the Mediterranean Fleet, based in Malta. Philip flew to the island in October and, while his ship underwent a refit, he stayed at the home of his uncle Dickie – Villa Guardamangia, a grand sandstone house with orange trees dotted throughout the gardens. A month later, on their second wedding anniversary, Princess Elizabeth flew out to join him, leaving one-year-old Prince Charles at home in the care of his grandparents. Upon Elizabeth's arrival, Dickie wrote to his younger daughter, Lady Pamela, saying, 'Lilibet is quite enchanting, and I've lost whatever of my heart is left to spare entirely to her.'

'It was a magic period of their early life,' Michael Parker, one of Philip's greatest friends and former private secretary, recalled. '[Elizabeth] had a ball. She had a wonderful time – we all went all over the island and visited people. She would have liked to have shopped but didn't. It wasn't the practice and it wasn't done. And she would be wearing all sorts of clothes the other wives were wearing. There was one particular dress – a black dress she wore. She looked stunning in it. They were a stunning couple – separately and together.'

It was in Malta that Dickie introduced Prince Philip to polo, which became his main sporting interest from then on. Not only was Dickie a first-class polo player, he also wrote the standard book on the sport. *An Introduction to Polo by 'Marco'* became the bible for polo players and was translated into Spanish and French.

Dickie remained a close friend to Prince Philip and Princess Elizabeth for the rest of his life, but it was with Prince Charles that Dickie formed the closest of friendships. When Prince Charles went to Cheam School in 1957, Dickie gave him as a Christmas present a subscription to the boys' weekly comic *Eagle*, in which Charles could follow the adventures of Dan Dare, Pilot of the Future, and his struggles with his arch nemesis the Mekon. *Eagle*, a comic based on Christian values, was launched in 1950 by Marcus Morris, an Anglican vicar who felt that the Church was not getting its message across to young people effectively. As such, it always maintained a high moral tone. Charles wrote to Dickie in thanks: 'I like *Eagle* very much. It has such exciting stories'. Charles continued to receive the comic every week until he was fifteen.

By the time Charles was a teenager, he had already started writing regularly to Dickie. While in Australia for two terms at Geelong Grammar School's Timbertop campus, he sent Dickie regular reports of his adventures in the outback and how he enjoyed his time there compared with the misery he experienced at Gordonstoun. Things changed for the better when he returned to Gordonstoun for a final term and was made Guardian (Head Boy) by Robert Chew, the headmaster. Charles wrote to Dickie: 'I don't know that I am doing my job very well as it is a rather vaguely defined one but I hope I shall get into the hang of it as the term goes on . . . I've come to the conclusion that I am not very good at organising people.'

In 1965, the Queen and the Duke of Edinburgh held a

dinner at Buckingham Palace to discuss Prince Charles's further education after leaving Gordonstoun. The guests included Prime Minister Harold Wilson, the Archbishop of Canterbury, the Dean of Windsor and Dickie Mountbatten. Wilson argued for a provincial university, but it was Dickie who persuaded Charles's parents that the right course would be from Trinity College, Cambridge, to Dartmouth naval college and then the Navy. It was agreed that Charles would live in college rooms at Trinity like any other undergraduate.

In July 1969, after the investiture of Prince Charles as Prince of Wales at Caernarfon Castle, Dickie wrote to him:

> Confidential reports of Naval Officers are summarised by numbers . . . poor 2 or 3 . . . very good 7 or 8 . . . your performance since you went with fleet coverage to Wales rates you a 9 in my opinion . . . I am sure you will keep your head. Realise how fickle public support can be – it has to be earned over again every year. Your Uncle David had such popularity he thought he could flout the Government and the Church and make a twice-divorced woman Queen. His popularity disappeared overnight. I am sure yours never will provided you keep your feet firmly on the ground.

He signed himself 'Your affectionate and admiring Uncle', as he had not yet been dubbed 'Honorary Grandfather' by Prince Charles, who himself became 'Honorary Grandson'.

In 1974, Dickie wrote to Charles giving him advice on

the subject of marriage: 'I believe that in a case like yours a man should sow his wild oats and have as many affairs as he can before settling down. But for a wife he should choose a suitable and sweet-charactered girl before she meets anyone else she might fall for.' He went on to say how suitable his granddaughter Amanda Knatchbull would be as a wife for Charles, describing her as 'incredibly affectionate and loyal with a glorious sense of fun and humour' and noting that 'she's a country girl as well which is even more important'. For the next five years Dickie would continue to press the case for Amanda, who had become close friends with Charles. When he eventually got round to proposing marriage to Amanda, she turned him down.

Mark Simpson, a former Buckingham Palace footman who sometimes assisted Prince Charles, remembered the Prince's relationship with Lord Mountbatten: 'They were certainly very close,' he told me, 'and I think Mountbatten was one of the very few people who would just say exactly what he thought the Prince should do and Prince Charles would do it.' When the Queen wasn't in residence at Windsor Castle, Prince Charles used to have Lord Mountbatten to stay on his own for the weekend. He stayed in a grand room just along from the Queen's sitting room. According to Simpson, Mountbatten was very charming and when he came in with all his bags he would help unpack them and chat to Simpson while doing so.

He and the Prince would have breakfast downstairs in the nursery and would then go outside with the red government dispatch boxes and briefcases. The footman remembers:

> We would set up a couple of card tables in the garden and some nice comfortable chairs. They sat by the aviary, which is just below the wall of the East Terrace, which is where Charles would sit on his own after Mountbatten died. They would sit looking over the lawn to Frogmore and work before having their lunch. This would be a cold salmon and salad and no alcohol, just jugs of Lemon Refresher as they chatted for hours. Lemon Refresher was a drink invented by Lord Mountbatten: a mixture of lemon juice, water and Epsom salts. Prince Charles always used to have a glass before he went to bed. The first thing I did every morning before laying the breakfast was to clear away the Lemon Refresher. They drank it all the time and it's supposed to be very good for you. I always had to remember to travel with it and not forget.
>
> They might have a swim in the afternoon; there is an indoor pool in the orangery and you can open up the glass doors, which all slide back. There was a cocktail cabinet in there and sun loungers, and when Mountbatten was staying, they would have dinner in the Queen's dining room – not black tie but cords and a blazer.

On 27 August 1979, Lord Mountbatten had been lobster fishing on his wooden boat, *Shadow V*, in the village of Mullaghmore, County Sligo, in the west of Ireland, where he had a holiday home. The Irish Republican Army had the night before planted a bomb on the boat. When it was remotely detonated, the boat was blown to pieces and Mountbatten, his teenage grandson Nicholas Knatchbull and fourteen-year-old deckhand Paul Maxwell from Enniskillen were killed instantly; Lady Brabourne, Dickie's eldest daughter's mother-in-law, died the following day from the injuries that she suffered in the attack.

Mark Simpson remembered the tragedy.

I was up at Balmoral when Mountbatten was killed. Prince Charles was fishing in Iceland or somewhere like that. All the staff were in shock and spoke in hushed whispers. The Queen drove over to Birkhall to tell Queen Elizabeth and everybody was terribly quiet. We were supposed to have our annual staff barbeque at Balmoral and they had been building a bonfire for days and days. Anyway, the word got around that the staff barbeque was cancelled and we weren't to have any staff entertainment at all. The staff canteen was shut down and everybody was terribly solemn. Then the royal family all went out on a barbeque themselves!

The incident caused public outrage and made news all around the world. Prince Charles was left devastated, after hearing the news while on a fishing trip to Iceland. That evening, he wrote in his journal:

A mixture of desperate emotions swept over me – agony, disbelief, a kind of wretched numbness, closely followed by fierce and violent determination to see that something was done about the IRA. Life will never be the same now that he has gone and I fear it will take me a very long time to forgive those people who today achieved something that two World Wars and thousands of Germans and Japanese failed to achieve.

He ended the entry by saying: 'I only hope I can live up to the expectations he had of me and be able to do something to honour the name of Mountbatten.'

Andrew Lownie, the author and historian, said: 'He was an honorary father, really. Prince Charles was a rather sensitive boy, and he showed him affection that his own father, the Duke of Edinburgh, never did.'

During a memorial service held to remember Mountbatten, Prince Charles gave an emotional address about the man he says had 'a constantly active brain which was never allowed a moment's rest'. He continued, 'Although he could certainly be ruthless with people when the occasion demanded, his infectious enthusiasm, his sheer capacity for hard work, his wit, made him an irresistible leader among men.'

Perhaps Prince Philip summed him up best of all when he said in a television interview, 'The world is made up of two types of people: those that complain but let things go on as they are and a small minority who say no and set the world on a new course.' The latter of which applied to his uncle.

After his brother George's premature death, Mountbatten

took his place as Philip's guardian, or at least that is how he saw himself. Later he would emphasise his role in raising the future royal consort and claim to have single-handedly engineered his romance with Princess Elizabeth.

Dickie's assassination may also have had the indirect result of pushing Charles to propose to Lady Diana Spencer. When they met a year after the funeral, Diana told Charles: 'You looked so sad when you walked up the aisle at Mountbatten's funeral. It was the most tragic thing I've ever seen. My heart bled for you when I watched. I thought, "You're so lonely – you should be with somebody to look after you."' Diana was later recorded on tape, as shown in the television documentary *Diana in Her Own Words*, stating that Charles 'leapt' on her after she said that. He finally proposed to Diana in February 1981, at Windsor Castle.

Besides his role as a friend, confidant and advisor to Philip and Charles, Dickie had had a glittering naval and military career. During the Second World War he was appointed Supreme Allied Commander South East Asia, and having driven the Japanese out of Burma he accepted the Japanese swords of surrender in Singapore on 12 September 1945. It was two years later that he was appointed Viceroy of India, the last person ever to carry that title. His job was to oversee the withdrawal of British rule. This was achieved but only through the partition of India and the creation of the new state of Pakistan, resulting in much bloodshed and the displacement of millions of people. 'I had a lot of criticism,' he said, 'and many thought I did a terrible job, which is unfair, but everything is unfair when it is based on inadequate knowledge.'

According to his biographer Philip Ziegler, Mountbatten's faults, like everything else about him, 'were on the grandest scale. His vanity, though child-like, was monstrous, his ambition unbridled . . . He sought to rewrite history with cavalier indifference to the facts to magnify his own achievements.' However, Ziegler concludes that Mountbatten's virtues outweighed his defects.

In 1953, he returned to the Royal Navy and a year later he was appointed First Sea Lord, the position that had been held by his father more than forty years before. Finally, in 1959, he became Chief of the Defence Staff, until in 1965 he retired from the Navy.

6

My Grandfather, King George VI

At first glance, King Charles III would appear to have little in common with his grandfather, King George VI. Their respective routes to the throne could not have been more different. Prince Albert – 'Bertie', as George VI was known to his family – was the second son of George V and had little prospect of becoming king. In fact, it was thought to be so unlikely that Bertie would accede to the throne that he was allowed to join the Royal Navy Air Corps when he was twenty-one, in 1916. Flying any type of early aircraft was highly risky; the life expectancy of pilots in the First World War was measured in weeks. But Bertie was considered expendable as he had two younger brothers who could fill his shoes as next-in-line if he had a fatal accident.

It was only due to the extraordinary turn of events that led to his brother's abdication that Bertie became the 'reluctant king'. When Edward informed Bertie that he had made up his mind to abdicate in order to marry Wallis Simpson, Bertie was horrified. According to the King's diary, Bertie said: 'That's a dreadful thing to hear, none of us wants that, I least of all.' His mother, Queen Mary, remembered how appalled he was at the news: 'He was devoted to his brother and the whole abdication crisis made him miserable. He sobbed on my shoulder for an hour.' He had a happy family life, with a wife he adored and two young daughters whom together he referred to as 'Us Four'. As the younger brother of the Prince of Wales, his royal duties had been relatively light. He knew that everything would change for the worse when he became King, a role for which he was totally unprepared, and he lacked the confidence that he would be able to handle his responsibilities successfully. He would have to leave the comfort of his family home at 145 Piccadilly and move into the vast and impersonal Buckingham Palace. Until now, he had enjoyed family holidays at Glamis Castle, his wife's parents' estate in Scotland, where informality was the order of the day. Instead, he would have to live with the much more formal atmosphere at Balmoral.

Prince Charles, in contrast, knew from an early age that he was destined to succeed to the throne. This set him apart from other boys at school, where a personal protection officer was always lurking in the background and made it difficult for him to fit in, at least until he went to Cambridge. Being king-in-waiting for so many years, he was able to learn from the example set by his mother as to what is involved in being monarch. He would have seen her deal with the daily red boxes of governmental papers, and in the last years of her reign he performed many royal duties on her behalf, including investitures and the opening of Parliament.

Prince Charles's grandfather, King George VI, was just fifty-six and had been expected to rule for many more years when he died suddenly of coronary thrombosis brought on by lung cancer in February 1952. Charles was only three years old when his grandfather died, but he had already been taught to bow before him.

Charles has claimed to have only one lasting memory of his grandfather. A souvenir brochure written for Charles's investiture as Prince of Wales in 1969 reveals that he 'vaguely recalls sitting with George VI to be photographed on his third birthday.' The text continues: 'In many ways the Prince of Wales resembles his grandfather, King George VI. He is reserved, quiet and afraid of hurting people's feelings.' At the time of his birth, Charles's mother was still a princess and not yet Queen. This meant that Charles was a grandson of the monarch through the female line rather than the male line and was therefore not eligible to be known as Prince Charles. However, the King intervened to make sure that Charles, as the son of a future queen and a future king himself, was created a prince.

While King George VI came abruptly to the throne without proper preparation for what was involved, he made sure that his daughter Princess Elizabeth, the heir apparent, suffered no such disadvantage. By the time she became Queen she had spent many hours at her father's side as he went through his red boxes and performed his duties as King. The Princess spent as much time as possible with her father, including accompanying him when he went shooting, when she would sit quietly beside him listening to his instructions on how to do this or that.

In spite of their very different routes to the throne, the lives of Prince Charles and his grandfather have a number of parallels. Bertie was born on 14 December 1895, a date that gave his parents some concern as it was known as 'Mausoleum Day' by Queen Victoria, being the anniversary of the death of her beloved husband Prince Albert of Saxe-Coburg-Gotha and the day on which she was usually in deepest mourning. However, when the infant was named Albert after his great-grandfather, Queen Victoria was delighted and sent a bust of her late husband to Bertie as a somewhat unusual christening present.

As a child, Bertie suffered from a number of physical ailments. Like his father before him, he suffered from knock knees, for which, from the age of eight, he was forced to wear splints on his legs for several hours during the day and when he went to bed at night. The splints had the desired effect and by the time he became King George VI, he had perfectly straight legs. He was also left-handed, which was considered 'curable' at that time, so the young Bertie was forced to write with his right hand. From an early age he also had a marked stammer, which was not helped by his father's impatience with him when he had trouble speaking. 'Get it out, boy!' he would order while Bertie struggled to form the words. His stammer made him nervous and shy and instilled in him a fear of public speaking.

When he was thirteen Bertie was sent to the Royal Naval College, Osborne, which was housed in the outbuildings and stable block of Queen Victoria's house on the Isle of Wight. As a naval cadet at Osborne, he suffered considerable pain with gastric complaints; in addition, his classmates nicknamed him 'Sardine' because of his diminutive stature. It was here that he met Surgeon-Lieutenant Louis Greig, the assistant medical officer who was to have such an important influence on Bertie's life. Greig was a keep-fit fanatic and was capped playing rugby for Scotland, who he captained several times. As a result, he was hero-worshipped by the cadets. The son of a merchant, he was brought up in Glasgow in a large family and studied medicine at Glasgow University. Greig was fifteen years older than Bertie but struck up a close friendship with the stuttering young man, so much so that Bertie gave Greig a present of a photograph of himself in a silver frame at the end of his first year.

Life at Osborne was spartan and not dissimilar to the regime at Prince Charles's school, Gordonstoun. The dormitories were cold in winter and the day started early with icy showers, now fashionably healthy. Everything was done at the double and keeping fit was a high priority. Despite the harshness of the conditions at the school, the King and Queen were impressed with the manner in which Greig treated their son through a series of illnesses, including whooping cough and influenza.

After three years at Osborne, Bertie went on to Dartmouth naval college to complete his training. When the time came for him to join his first ship in 1913, his father King George V arranged for him to be assigned to HMS *Cumberland*, where Louis Greig was the ship's surgeon. Later that year, with war seeming ever more likely, Bertie and Greig were separated when Greig joined the Marines. He was taken prisoner in Belgium in 1914. After eight months in a prisoner-of-war camp, Greig was exchanged for a German doctor. On his return he was summoned to an audience with King George V, who asked Greig to take care of Bertie, whose naval career had been interrupted by spells of sick leave. It was Greig who persuaded Bertie to have an operation on a duodenal ulcer, against the advice of the King's more cautious physicians. The operation was a success and Greig was rewarded by the King, being made a member of the Royal Victorian Order.

With his physical problems behind him, Prince Albert became a keen sportsman. He excelled at lawn tennis and in 1920 won the RAF doubles competition playing with Greig. They also appeared in the men's doubles at Wimbledon in 1926, where they were beaten in the first round by a couple of veteran players who between them had won numerous championships. Bertie also became a competent horseman and rode to hounds throughout the season, until 1931, when the Civil List was reduced and economies had to be found.

Bertie decided that the Navy was not for him and instead signed up with the Auxiliary Air Force, which later became the Royal Air Force. At the request of the King, Greig went as Bertie's equerry to RAF College Cranwell, where they lived in the same house and took flying lessons. Bertie had just earned his pilot's licence when the war ended, after which he was promoted to squadron leader. However, he was grounded when the King decided that Bertie and his younger brother Prince Henry Duke of Gloucester should go up to Trinity College, Cambridge. As the King did not want his sons living in lodgings with the other undergraduates, he rented a large house for Greig, who was by then a married man with a daughter. Bertie and Henry moved in with the Greigs, which gave them the experience of living with an ordinary, middle-class family. The brothers wanted motorcycles to get around Cambridge but the King was against it, saying: 'Only bounders ride motor bicycles.' Greig was able to persuade him otherwise and the brothers each acquired a 'snorter', as they were known.

At Cambridge, Bertie and his brother had little opportunity to mix with other undergraduates as the King had instructed Greig to keep a close eye on them. They socialised with their cousin Lord Louis Mountbatten, an undergraduate at Christ's College, who was five years younger than Bertie and who later became aide-de-camp to Edward, the Prince of Wales. After a year, Bertie left Cambridge without sitting for a degree but he did learn much about the British Constitution and the nature of monarchy, a subject in which he became an acknowledged expert.

Unlike his elder brother the Prince of Wales, who enjoyed the company of many ladies both single and married, Bertie was a slow starter with girlfriends. Although good-looking and personable, his stammer made him shy when it came to approaching girls. Bertie was first formally introduced to Lady Elizabeth Bowes-Lyon at a dinner party on Derby night, 1920, in Grosvenor Square. He was immediately captivated by the vivacious, attractive and aristocratic debutante, who was to be presented to the King and Queen at Holyroodhouse later that year. Bertie joined the social scene so that he could see more of her and decided she was the only woman he would ever marry. She was not of the same mind, however, and rejected his proposal of marriage twice before finally accepting in 1923. Greig had proved himself the matchmaker by persuading Bertie not to give up in the face of the refusals. Bertie, who by then had been made Duke of York, had appointed Greig as comptroller of his household.

Two years later, Bertie engaged the services of speech therapist Lionel Logue, who had heard him deliver a painfully slow and halting speech at the closing of the British Empire Exhibition at Wembley Stadium in 1925. Thanks to Logue, the Prince's speech impediment was eventually cured and he found a new self-confidence in all areas of his life. In 1927, he went on a six-month tour of the southern hemisphere, culminating in his opening of the Australian parliament. He delivered his speech without hesitation and afterwards wrote to his father King George V: 'I have so much more confidence in myself now, which I am sure comes from being able to speak properly at last.'

Bertie took part in all forms of blood sports. As well as hunting, which he had to give up for safety reasons on acceding to the throne, he enjoyed fishing and deer stalking at Balmoral and wildfowling on the Norfolk fens. His favourite sport was shooting, at which he was particularly adept. He kept a meticulous game book, from his first shoot at the age of twelve at Sandringham until the day before his death, recording his own kills in red ink. The passion for shooting has run in the royal family for generations – fourteen gamekeepers are employed at Sandringham to ensure that the shooting is some of the best in England.

Throughout his life Bertie kept notes of all his ailments and of the medicines and treatments he received. Although, as King, he had the advice of the most eminent medical men in the country, he was a fervent believer in homeopathy, an interest he shared with his grandmother, Queen Alexandra. Dr John Weir, who was appointed one of the King's official physicians in 1937, was the first president of the Faculty of Homeopathy. Bertie named one of his homebred racehorses Hypericum, after the homeopathic remedy derived from St John's wort.

In the end, neither his doctors nor any alternative remedies could save King George VI from the effects of a lifetime of heavy smoking, which resulted in his having an operation to remove his lung in September 1951. On the day before he died, in February 1952, he went shooting on the Sandringham estate. Lord Fermoy, the former Member of Parliament for King's Lynn, who was in the party of six guns, which bagged no fewer than 300 hares, described it as a 'perfectly marvellous day' when speaking to the *Lynn News and Advertiser*. 'The King was a great shot and was on the top of his form. I saw him get nine hares and even one pigeon which he took perfectly cleanly 80 to 100 feet up.' Recalling the moments at the end of the shoot, Lord Fermoy said: 'The King hurried round and asked us to come again on Thursday. The estate looked lovely and the King really enjoyed his day.'

Just after 7.30 a.m. the following morning, James MacDonald, the King's valet, came into his rooms with his morning tea and found him dead. It was discovered he had suffered a coronary thrombosis and had died quietly in his sleep.

As a child, Prince Charles, too, had some health problems. He was prone to catching colds, which led to chronic sinus infections; he had his tonsils out when he was eight years old; at Cheam, his first boarding school, he was unco-ordinated and overweight, which may have contributed to his lack of success at games. He was unsuited to the regime of cold showers and freezing dormitories. His father Prince Philip wrongly thought that the rigours of Gordonstoun school would toughen him up. Instead, he had a miserable time there and suffered from bullying. In 1966, at the age of seventeen, Charles went to school in Australia for two terms, which he found more to his liking. When he returned, he took up polo and received yachting lessons from his father. Like Bertie, he was also keen on hunting, fishing and shooting – until persuaded by Princess Diana to give up the mass slaughter of game birds. He learned to fly jet aircraft with the RAF and took annual skiing holidays in Klosters, Switzerland. Such was his sporting prowess that he was dubbed 'Action Man' by the British press.

Like his grandfather, Prince Charles became a lifelong believer in, and supporter of, homeopathy. In 1993, he launched a controversial charity, the Prince's Foundation for Integrated Health. Its aims were to promote alternative medicines, including homeopathy, and have them made available on the National Health Service. It failed after a number of years; medical opinion based on clinical trials said that there was no evidence of any beneficial effect from these medicines, and the charity was wound up amid allegations of fraud and money laundering.

Both Bertie and Prince Charles had a particular interest in helping young people from underprivileged backgrounds. In 1919, Bertie became president of the Boys' Industrial Welfare Association, which had been set up to improve working conditions for boys in industry. One of his initiatives, and by far the most popular, was the setting up of the Duke of York's Camp. As a social experiment, the camps enabled boys from different backgrounds to get to know each other and were held annually from 1919 until the outbreak of the Second World War. Some 400 boys, half from public schools and half from industry, were invited to spend a week together in the countryside. The boys played sports at the camp, where food and accommodation were provided free of charge. Each year Bertie would spend a day with them, joining in the activities and leading a sing-song in the evening. The final camp was held at Balmoral in 1939, where the boys were guests of the King.

Almost forty years later, in 1976, Prince Charles finished

his tour of duty with the Royal Navy and he set up the Prince's Trust with the idea of helping disadvantaged young people in the UK. It was funded with private donations, including the Prince's own severance pay from the Navy. It has since grown into a worldwide group of organisations giving young people everywhere a chance to get on in life, both by helping them to become independent with grants to set up new businesses and by setting up activity schemes for them to gain confidence and realise their potential. By 2020 the Trust was able to announce that it had helped more than 1 million young people.

King George VI did not live long enough to see his grandchildren reach adulthood, but he did delight in the company of little Charles, who spent some time with him and the Queen while Princess Elizabeth and Philip were travelling. Just after Charles's first birthday, on her second wedding anniversary in November 1949, Princess Elizabeth flew to Malta to join her husband. Charles and his nanny Helen Lightbody were put in the care of his grandparents, who were to spend Christmas at Sandringham. 'Charles is too sweet stumping around the room,' the King wrote to his daughter in Malta. 'We shall love having him at Sandringham. He is the fifth generation to live there and I hope he will get to love the place.'

Charles was only three and staying at Sandringham with his grandparents, his little sister Anne and his aunt Princess Margaret when his grandfather died, on 6 February 1952. Dutiful as ever, Queen Elizabeth wrote a sensitive letter of sympathy to her mother-in-law, Queen Mary, from Sandringham:

> It is impossible for me to grasp what has happened. Last night he was in wonderful form and looking so well and this morning, only a few hours ago, I was sent a message that his servant couldn't wake him. I flew to his room and thought he was in a deep sleep, he looked so peaceful – and then I realised what had happened. It is hard to grasp, he was such an angel to the children and me and I cannot bear to think of Lilibet, so young to bear such a burden. I do feel for you darling Mama – to lose two dear sons and Bertie so young still, and so precious – it is almost more than one can bear.

The 'so young' Lilibet her mother spoke of was only twenty-five when her father died. She had two children: Prince Charles, who would be four in November of that year, and Princess Anne, who would be two in August. It was the end of her hopes of the 'hands-on' motherhood she had envisaged enjoying with her children. Self-control – iron, unflagging, superhuman self-control – was to be the order of the day. The new Queen believed that indulging in emotion of any kind could deflect her from the cool performance she needed to put on in public and private. In 1952 women were considered suitable for the home and hearth, not for positions of power and influence. Her father, having observed these characteristics in his daughter, knew that when she became Queen, she would take things steadily, which would enable her to do the job of being a woman in a man's world that much better. Unlike him, she was meticulous and swift, and unlike him she did not appear so thoughtful and loving, because she suppressed rather than expressed her feelings.

It was sad that Charles was too young to know his grandfather as, had he done so, he would have had a very different role model from his own father. Charles might have been introduced to his future role in a gentler, kinder way instead of the assault course he was eventually subjected to, which was only alleviated when Camilla returned to his life.

7

MY GRANDMOTHER, THE QUEEN MOTHER

From the day she became a young widow in February 1952 until the day she died just over fifty years later, Queen Elizabeth the Queen Mother was a powerful if underestimated influence on her daughter's reign. Family decisions always took into consideration what 'Mummy' would think, and – in almost all cases – if it was decided she might be opposed, the idea was instantly shelved.

When there were discussions about moving the workings of the Royal Ascot Enclosure office from its home in St James's Palace, both the Queen and Princess Margaret vetoed the plan. However extravagant it was to run such an antiquated system – for security reasons, the Royal Enclosure badges had to be collected from St James's in person – they were adamant it must remain. Its removal to a more appropriate place, on the racecourse, 'would upset Mummy terribly', they agreed. It duly stayed in situ until after her death. Both the Queen and Margaret were saddened by the death of royal couturier Norman Hartnell in 1979, but their first concern was, 'Who is going to make Mummy's clothes now?'

The late Diana, Princess of Wales had no illusions about the Queen Mother and the great sway she held, especially over Prince Charles. 'He was in awe of his Grandmama and I was always the third person in the room,' she explained. 'It was always "Mummy, would you like a drink? Granny, would you like a drink?"' When William was christened on 4 August 1982, the date had been chosen to coincide with the Queen Mother's birthday. 'Nobody asked me when it was suitable for William – 11 o'clock couldn't have been worse,' Diana made clear. 'Endless pictures of the Queen, the Queen Mother, Charles and William. I was totally excluded.' The Princess also hated the performance Charles put on when greeting his grandmother: he would kiss her hand in a gentlemanly way but then place kisses all the way up her arm with a theatrical flourish.

Diana knew the Queen Mother was distrustful of her and that she suspected Diana of being incapable of telling the truth. 'She is not as she appears at all,' Diana told me firmly in the summer of 1997. 'She is tough and interfering and has few feelings.' There are no surviving letters between the two women, as Princess Margaret destroyed much of her mother's controversial correspondence, which included letters from Diana. This destruction of history was witnessed and aided by her chauffeur at the time, David Griffin, and her police protection officer John

Harding. Some of the correspondence was burned and some was shredded. There is virtually no mention of the failing marriage between Charles and Diana in William Shawcross's official biography of the Queen Mother – presumably because there was nothing left to refer to.

It is well known that Prince Charles sought solace with his grandmother during those impossible years. The chats were 'closed meetings' and none of the staff, even the Queen Mother's much-loved Page of the Backstairs, Billy Tallon, were privy to what was said. The Queen Mother had a wonderful way of dealing with things she did not want to discuss, greeting any such topic with a simple 'Some things are better left unsaid.' Diana's name was no longer mentioned in front of the Queen Mother, even though her and Charles's marriage dramas were on the lips of everyone at the time.

There was also no mention of the Queen's irritation that her son took his most pressing problems to his grandmother instead of to her. He continued to do so for the rest of her life, not because he didn't love his mother, but because she had never shown him the sort of affection and under-standing that his grandmother did. The Queen and Charles's relationship was very formal and nothing like the close bond he had with his grandmother. It wasn't until much later in both their lives that Charles formed any proper connection of this kind with his mother.

When Diana was tragically killed a few weeks after the Queen Mother's ninety-seventh birthday, the latter was staying at Balmoral Castle along with Charles, William and Harry. She had witnessed the misery the breakdown of the marriage had caused her grandson, as well as the struggles it was now causing his boys, who were having to divide their holidays between their mother and father. Prince William loved Balmoral and had been longing to leave the madness surrounding their St Tropez holiday with the Al Fayed family for the peace of the Scottish estate.

From her Scottish outpost the Queen Mother was kept up to date with the outpourings of grief surrounding Diana's death by her good friend Maureen, Marchioness of Dufferin and Ava, who was a famous hostess in her time and still lived in some splendour in Hans Crescent by Harrods. Maureen explained to the bewildered Queen Mother that things felt 'very odd' in London and people who had never known or met Diana were placing flowers, still in their cellophane wrapping, outside Kensington and Buckingham Palaces. There was also an air of disquiet in the city and she thought the Queen Mother should know. Maureen's description of growing public resentment towards the royal family worried the Queen Mother. 'To think that Diana caused more trouble in death than she did in life,' she said with more than a touch of bitterness. It was a niggling concern to her that the younger members of the royal family, in their short tenure, had managed to behave so badly. She felt they had destroyed a lot of the good she and King George VI had done during the war and that subsequently her daughter, the Queen, had worked so hard to preserve.

The Queen Mother was certainly not the gentle old lady of popular imagination but a force to be reckoned with, every bit as powerful in her later years as she was in her youth. Her strength had enabled her to guide George VI through the rigours of a life he never wanted or expected. By her resolve she strengthened the backbone of her stuttering, self-conscious husband and made him an effective wartime leader and king. Prince Charles paid tribute to her capability, confirming that she had 'an immensely strong character, combined with a unique natural grace and an infectious optimism about life itself.' He went on to explain how she 'understood the British character', which of course she did only too well, causing Adolf Hitler to make his famous remark about her being 'the most dangerous woman in Europe'.

Charles also stressed how much his grandmother had meant to everyone in the family, 'particularly the Queen, to whom she was such a stalwart and sensitive support when my grandfather died'. Princess Elizabeth was only twenty-five and needed a mother's guidance when, in 1952, she was propelled into a male-dominated world where women counted for little – and yet there she was, as Queen. She and Philip were in Kenya when the King died in Norfolk, and they didn't hear the news until hours later. The soon-to-be Queen Mother and Princess Margaret were at Sandringham, having dined with the King while their grandchildren, three-year-old Prince Charles and one-and-a-half-year-old Princess Anne, were tucked up in bed in the nursery. Much to her frustration, the Queen Mother had no way of contacting her daughter as the telephone service from England to Kenya was intermittent and only open a few hours a day.

When Elizabeth, who was now Queen, eventually heard the news, she was icy-calm and – as frequently happens with a tremendous shock – she robotically took charge of proceedings. The royal journey home involved driving through the bush from the lodge where they were staying to a local airport that had a proper runway but was not equipped for use after dark. A tropical thunderstorm delayed them at their next stop, the Ugandan city of Entebbe, from which they eventually departed at midnight for the twenty-hour flight to London (including fuelling stops). She refused to think about the reality of how much her life was about to change and instead worried for her 21-year-old sister, Margaret. She knew her mother would be able to take it all in her capable stride – that is, if she wanted to do so, and if not, she would simply retire to her bed.

When Princess Elizabeth was growing up, her mother had been a remote, rather magisterial figure. She was an affectionate enough presence when she was there, but as soon as the clarion of 'duty' called she would be gone again, sometimes for months on end. Elizabeth and Margaret spent their young lives having to get to know her all over again when she returned from yet another long absence.

By the standards of her class and the times, though, Queen Elizabeth (previously Duchess of York) was a dutiful mother who devoted time and attention to her children. Certainly, enough love was generated in those early years to ensure that, once they were adults, she formed the closest of friendships with her namesake, whom she called Lilibet, and her younger daughter, Margaret Rose. The three women grew to prefer each other's company to anyone else's. They holidayed together by royal tradition but also out of choice. They gossiped to each other on the telephone every day – sometimes in French – and the switchboard operators at Buckingham Palace took particular delight in saying, as they put the Queen Mother through to the Queen, 'Your Majesty? Her Majesty, Your Majesty.' They also enjoyed lunch together when their royal duties allowed. While their conversations revolved around various subjects, horse racing and family matters were prominent among them. The Queen Mother did have strong views on certain topics, one of which was her vehement opposition to the idea that the Duke and Duchess of Windsor should ever return to live in England.

The three also delighted in letting their hair down (in old age the Queen Mother's hair, when it was unfurled, reached almost to her waist). All were partial to a stiff Martini or two, which could sometimes lead to scenes more suited to a *Carry On* film than the studious decorum of their public images. One Christmas at Sandringham they got through nearly a whole bottle of gin, and another of Dubonnet, before dinner. When they eventually made it to the table in the dining room, the Queen Mother could not get the vegetables out of the silver serving dish that the stoic-faced footman was holding. Spoonfuls of peas were sent cascading to the floor, accompanied by regal peels of high-pitched, inebriated laughter.

Such intimacy had to wait until her daughters were grown up, however. All Queen Elizabeth wanted for the two girls as children, she said in summary, was for them 'to spend as long as possible in the open air, to enjoy to the full the pleasures of the country, to be able to dance and draw and appreciate music, to acquire good manners and perfect deportment, and to cultivate all the distinctive feminine graces.'

The Princesses' governess, Marion Crawford, remarked: 'I often had the feeling that the Duke and Duchess, most happy in their own married life, were not over-concerned with the higher education of their daughters.' What was important was a sense of propriety, and there to ensure that it was instilled at as early an age as possible were the Duchess's formidable in-laws, Queen Mary and King George V. Both were sticklers for doing everything very strictly by the book and their own children had been brought up in an atmosphere of stifling formality. By the time their grandchildren arrived, age had leavened their approach, but not by very much. Hugs and kisses were never a feature of the royal family's parental agenda and their emotional strictures were carried through into the next generation. This goes a long way to explaining some of the problems that have continued to beset the family in recent years.

Had the young Duchess been left to bring up her daughters in her own way, the two girls, and Lilibet in particular, might have enjoyed a more relaxed childhood than they did. But their warm-hearted mother was not in charge of her own destiny, or indeed that of either of her children. King George V and Queen Mary dictated how their granddaughters were raised, and when Queen Mary said she was going to visit a museum or an exhibition and asked if her granddaughters might like to accompany her, the 'suggestion' was taken as a royal command. Under her watchful eye, Lilibet was taught to smile for the photographers, wave to the crowd and control her bladder in return for the reward of a biscuit. 'Teach that child not to fidget,' Queen Mary ordered, and to ensure that she did not, the pockets of the little Princess Elizabeth's dresses were sewn up. All this before she was three years old.

The Duchess of York might well have resented her in-laws' dominating influence, but if she did she was careful to keep her thoughts to herself. Her behaviour must be viewed in context, however: what would seem bizarre and decidedly uncaring to later generations was accepted as perfectly normal at the time – and the Duchess was always of her Edwardian time. She had married into a family that was governed by its own rules and, never one to court confrontation if it could possibly be avoided, she simply gave in. The daughter of an earl, she had been brought up by her own family to believe in rank and due deference.

In 1927, when she left the nine-month-old Lilibet and set off with her husband on a six-month-long world tour, she was generally applauded for doing her wifely duty. Even so, the parting was not an easy one. She was in such floods of tears when she left her baby daughter that the car taking her to the station to catch the train to Portsmouth – where she would embark on the battle cruiser HMS *Renown* – had to be driven around and around until she composed herself enough to face the waiting crowd. There would be more tears when she came home again, though this time they were Lilibet's. The infant had frustrated all her nursemaid Alah's efforts to get her to say 'Mother' or even 'Mama', and she clung pathetically to her nanny's skirts before eventually being prized loose to join the Duchess on the balcony of Buckingham Palace. It was hardly an auspicious return and the Duchess immediately set about establishing a proper home for Lilibet.

The York family moved out of the Queen Mother's father's, the Earl of Strathmore's, town house in Bruton Street, just off Berkeley Square in Mayfair, which had been their London base since Bertie and Elizabeth's wedding, and into a large mansion at 145 Piccadilly overlooking Hyde Park Corner. The King gave them Royal Lodge in Windsor Great Park for their weekend retreat, and a well-ordered routine was established, with Alah at the helm.

At 7.30 a.m. the nanny would get the girls out of bed and give them breakfast in the top-floor nursery before taking them downstairs to spend all of fifteen minutes with their parents. The morning was spent at lessons with Marion Crawford, with a break at 11 a.m. for a biscuit and a glass of orangeade, before a light lunch at 1.15 p.m. The afternoons were spent outside or, if it happened to be raining, drawing, learning to sew and knit, and studying music. They were given afternoon tea at 4.45 p.m. Their mother, if she happened to be in London, would join them in the nursery at 5.30 p.m. for an hour's play and reading. Supper followed and then, at 7.15 p.m. on the dot, they were put to bed. Encouraged by his wife, the Duke would sometimes break with the convention of the time, which all but barred fathers from the nursery floor, and join them on bath nights.

The routine was safe, methodical, disciplined – and sometimes lonely. Marion Crawford arrived at 145 Piccadilly when Princess Elizabeth was five years old. 'Until I came, she had never been allowed to get dirty,' the governess later recalled. 'Life had consisted of drives in the park, or quiet ladylike games in Hamilton Gardens, keeping to the paths; or leisurely drives around London in an open carriage, waving graciously to people when Alah told her to.' Crawfie, as the Princesses called her, introduced her young charges to games of hide-and-seek and 'Red Indians'. She took them for a ride on the top floor of a double-decker bus and, once, on the Underground to Tottenham Court Road. She even allowed them to get themselves dirty, just as their mother had done when she was little.

But as with their mother when she was a child, ordinary

companions of their own age were most notable by their absence. Their best friends were either chosen for them, or they were their toys. Lilibet had a large collection of foot-high model horses that she stabled in the nursery landing. 'Other children always had an enormous fascination, like mystic beings from a different world, and the little girls used to smile shyly at those they liked the look of,' Crawford remembered. 'They would have loved to speak to them and make friends, but this was never encouraged. They seldom had other children to tea.' The governess thought that 'a pity'. It is doubtful if their mother thought about it at all.

The death of George V and the abdication of Edward VIII changed the situation completely. The family moved out of Piccadilly into Buckingham Palace; the new King and Queen took up the reins of responsibility (he hesitantly, she with a will) and embarked on a series of foreign tours. Queen Mary continued to exert her influence from the shadows and life for the Princesses carried on very much as before. When war broke out and the country their father reigned over fought for its existence, Princesses Elizabeth and Margaret Rose lived in the comparative safety of Windsor Castle. Since the age of sixteen, when she had registered with the local Labour Exchange at Windsor, as the law required, Princess Elizabeth had badgered and pleaded with her father to be allowed to join one of the women's services. 'I ought to do as other girls of my own age do,' she said.

It was not until she reached eighteen, however, that she was allowed to enrol in the Auxiliary Territorial Service as 2nd Subaltern Elizabeth Windsor and learn how to adjust a carburettor and drive a truck. By then the war was all but over and the dangers George VI had been so anxious that his daughter should avoid were almost past. What that meant in effect was that the aloof and introverted Elizabeth was never given the chance to mix with girls of her own age, to share in their privations, to broaden her outlook. The King's attitude was understandable. Brought up in a self-contained family that made a point of avoiding exposure to competition and scrutiny, and pessimistic by nature, he saw his public obligations as a burden rather than an opportunity or a challenge, and it was his urgent wish to shield his daughter from those same predestined responsibilities for as long as possible.

Queen Elizabeth's reasons for deferring to her husband on a matter so vital to her daughter's development were more complex. The maternal desire to protect her offspring played its obvious part, as did her old-fashioned notion of a wife's duty, which dictated that a husband have the final say. But more than that, it is indicative of how deeply she had been absorbed into the royal family. It had involved compromise, concession, application, the surrender of certain maternal rights and adherence to a strict code of conduct. It meant cutting herself off from her own family. But that was a price she was happy to pay – as the Duchess of Windsor had been quick to note, Elizabeth liked being

royal. It afforded her everything she wanted from life: position, respect, esteem and the opportunity to do something
of value. It meant she never really had to think about money,
which was just as well, because throughout her life Queen
Elizabeth spent it lavishly. Perhaps most important of all,
it allowed her to create for herself a secure and comfortable
setting in which change was only an occasional visitor,
standards of a bygone age could be maintained and the
day-to-day problems of ordinary life could be kept firmly
in their place. Seamless continuity was what counted; what
the King wanted and what her royal parents-in-law had
demanded was good enough for her and, in turn, for her
daughters.

The Queen was not completely supportive of Princess
Elizabeth's desire to marry Prince Philip, partly because
she and the King thought their daughter was too young
to marry and hoped she might change her mind. It was
for this reason that they took her on their five-month tour
of South Africa in 1947, to give her more time to think
about getting engaged. When the engagement was
announced, on 10 July 1947, the Queen wrote to Tommy
Lascelles, the King's private secretary: 'You can imagine
what emotion this engagement has given me. It is one of
the things that has been in the forefront of all one's hopes
and plans for a daughter who has such a burden to carry,
and one can only pray that she has made the right decision.
I think she has – but he [Philip] is untried as yet.'

After the wedding the Queen wrote effusively to her
daughter about how happy she and the King were in

Elizabeth's happiness, and how they 'both love Philip already as a son'. She wrote that she looked forward to having just as much fun as before, even now that 'we four' had become 'we five'.

When, eight years after the King's death, the issue of Princess Margaret's blossoming passion for his former equerry Peter Townsend reared its head, only the Queen Mother emerged from the crisis unscathed. This hands-off attitude was typical of her style. Whenever a crisis confronted her, she would turn away or retire to bed with a psychosomatic illness brought on by the stress. The problem, she declared, was for her elder daughter, as Queen, to resolve. The Queen Mother remained serenely detached. It was an approach more befitting a grandmother than it ever was a mother – and grandmother was a part to which she was far better suited. Indeed, looking at the bright, smiling, sympathetic figure that strode the nation's stage for the next five decades, it is hard to imagine her as anything else.

Like a lot of women, Queen Elizabeth made a better grandmother than she did a mother. With the Queen pre-occupied and often overwhelmed by her sovereign duties, and Prince Philip determinedly pursuing first his naval career and then his own endeavours, it was the Queen Mother who stepped in to fill the emotional gap. Her help was certainly needed. The Queen, observed Godfrey Talbot, the BBC's court correspondent at the time, 'had been trained since the cradle by her father that duty came before everything, including family. She reluctantly had to abandon her family and they virtually didn't see their parents for months on end. During the first years of the Queen's reign the Queen Mother was both mother and father.'

In October 1950, Queen Elizabeth wrote to her mother-in-law Queen Mary after having her grandchildren to stay: 'Charles is really too angelic and such a clever child. His memory is prodigious and he takes a deep interest in everything. He is such a friendly little boy and everyone loves him.'

After Christmas that same year she wrote to her daughter Princess Elizabeth, who was in Malta, that 'I can't tell you how sweet he was driving to the station before Xmas . . . He was thrilled with the tree and after gazing at it tried to punch the silver balls and then had great fun helping to unpack everyone else's parcels.'

She had a similar role to that which Queen Mary had fulfilled a generation earlier, but unlike her demanding mother-in-law, the Queen Mother was happy to allow the children to develop at their own pace, in their own way, without bringing any undue pressure to bear on her charges. Rules and regulations had to be maintained, of course. When Charles was 'incarcerated' – as he put it – at Gordonstoun (against his grandmother's wishes; she wanted him to go to Eton), he would seek weekend refuge with his grandmother at Birkhall, her home on the Balmoral estate, which was about 75 miles from Gordonstoun. He adored it there. It was, he said, 'a unique haven of cosiness and character where the tea table was laden with freshly baked cakes and the log fires kept everyone snug winter and summer'. When he pleaded not to be sent back to Gordonstoun, however, the Queen Mother gently but firmly sent him on his way, with the inevitable reminder: 'All good things must come to an end.' She knew it was not her place to interfere, but she did sometimes take him back late to school, explaining to the housemaster, 'You know what grannies are like. Half the fun of being a grandmother is being able to spoil your grandchildren.'

Later, in 1966, when the Queen Mother was on tour in Australia, she was able to meet Prince Charles while he was a student at Geelong Grammar School's Timbertop campus. Princess Margaret wrote to her mother saying she was so happy that she and Charles could be together, 'for I have never known a grandson more devoted than Charles is to you'. This devotion began at a very young age; according to his biographer Jonathan Dimbleby, Charles had been taught early on to bow and kiss hands when he entered the presence of the King and Queen, but was nonetheless encouraged to clamber onto the Queen's lap, where, cuddled in her arms, he would listen with rapt attention as she told him stories. In adulthood he regarded his own parents as literary philistines, which wasn't quite true, but certainly neither of them shared his passion for opera, ballet and classical music, nor did they have his understanding of Shakespeare, all of which he was taught to appreciate by his grandmother. In an interview with the radio station Classic FM, Charles recalled that the first time he really became aware of music was when he was 'taken by my grandmother, Queen Elizabeth, to Covent

Garden – aged seven, I think. It must have been in 1956, to see the Bolshoi Ballet perform. It was their first visit to the United Kingdom and I shall never forget that incredible occasion. I was completely inspired by it.'

Charles also inherited his grandmother's love for gardens and the countryside and activities such as fishing, shooting and deer stalking. As a child, the Queen Mother had learned the rudiments of fishing for trout at her parents' ancestral home, Glamis Castle. Later in life she became a highly skilful angler. Mrs McKee, the royal cook at Balmoral, said that 'her great passion was for salmon fishing and this she did with intense concentration for hours on end. She would put on waders and old clothes and attempt to catch the biggest salmon she could find. She liked no interruption and took with her only the simplest of cold picnics.' The Queen Mother displayed her trademark sense of humour when, in 1982, she was rushed to hospital after a fishbone became stuck in her throat and she had to have an operation to remove it. She joked afterwards that 'the salmon have got their own back'.

Charles's own passion for fishing meant that his grandmother was able to pass on to him useful tips for fishing in the River Muick, which leads to the River Dee from the royal estate at Birkhall. Speaking of Birkhall in an interview with *Country Life*, the King described it as 'such a special place, particularly because it was made by my grandmother. It is a childhood garden and all I've done really is enhance it a bit. It's crucial to keep places that link generations, or we simply lose touch.'

There was a certain selectivity in the Queen Mother's approach to her grandchildren, it must be said. She doted on Prince Charles, as she did on Princess Margaret's son, David Linley, now Lord Snowdon, and his sister, Lady Sarah Chatto. She was more circumspect in her dealing with Princes Andrew and Edward, but only because the Queen, by then more comfortable in her role of Sovereign, had afforded them more time than she had their two elder siblings. Only Princess Anne was immune to her charm and then only for a while. She explained it thus: 'The Queen Mother is a wonderful family person and when I was a child and up to my teens, I don't think I went along with the family bit, so my appreciation of my grandmother probably developed later than anybody else's.' Another explanation might be that, as usual, the males drew more out from the Queen Mother. But all her grandchildren at one time or another felt moved to comment on how much comfort and affection she had given them. It was a role she made her own until the end of her life. She provided them, as Prince Charles said, 'with fun, laughter, warmth and infinite security'.

After her death, in 2002, Prince Charles paid tribute to the Queen Mother in a broadcast to the nation. He described her as 'the original life enhancer – at once indomitable, somehow timeless, able to span generations. Wise, loving, with an utterly irresistible mischievousness of spirit, above all she understood the British character and her heart belonged to this ancient old land and its equally indomitable and humorous inhabitants.'

He praised her for seeing the funny side of life, saying: 'We laughed till we cried and, oh, how I shall miss those laughs . . . She had wisdom and sensitivity, too, and she was quite simply the most magical grandmother you could possibly have.'

8

MY FATHER, PRINCE PHILIP

When Prince Philip, the Duke of Edinburgh, died in April 2021, the media was full of praise for his many accomplishments. Newspaper supplements, television programmes and commentators detailed a lifetime of achievements in glowing terms, in particular his ceaseless public support of the Queen in his position as consort. Equal praise was heaped on his work for the World Wildlife Fund and for conservation, his constant support for all things British (particularly in the field of engineering), his support for young people with his Duke of Edinburgh's Award scheme, his work with the military as Captain General of the Royal Marines and other regiments, and his patronage of more than 600 charitable organisations. Considerably less was said about his personal family life, as a husband to the Queen and as a father to four children, including his eldest son Prince Charles, with whom he had a difficult relationship for many years.

In order to better understand Prince Philip's family

relationships, it is necessary to examine the kind of man he was outside of his public persona. He was a man of many outstanding qualities: intelligent, dutiful, hard-working and capable of making a success out of anything he turned his hand to. He also had his faults: sometimes brusque and impatient to the point of rudeness, he was said to be unemotional and insensitive, particularly when it came to his relationship with Charles. While he enjoyed discussing myriad subjects, he would never admit to losing an argument, even if deep down he knew he was wrong.

He had a degree of self-belief that sometimes amounted to conceit. In his mind he was always right. The Queen acknowledged this as far as their children were concerned, as her father's illness and premature death in 1952 meant she had to resume her royal duties towards the end of Charles's first year and had only minimal parental involve-ment during his infancy – she left it to Philip to have the final word on how best to bring up their son, even if she didn't always wholeheartedly agree. Out of necessity, the Queen was expressing a long-distance affection, or love at arm's length, which Charles would come to believe was acceptable. Philip expected his children to stand on their own two feet, just as he'd had to do. In the words of Graham Turner in his biography of Elizabeth, 'The Queen left the children to Philip and Philip left them to life.'

Both the Queen and Prince Philip seemed rather dispas-sionate and uninvolved as parents. They usually didn't know what their children were doing. If any of the children had a problem, they didn't talk it through with them. Neither children nor parents expected to have much to do with one another's private lives. They didn't have much common ground and they never developed the habit of talking to each other except about the most trivial of things. 'Both Charles and Anne had an old-fashioned aristocratic upbringing,' recalled Lord Charteris, who worked at the palace from 1950 to 1977 as Elizabeth's private secretary. 'It was a complete time warp. They never talked about their difficulties. The Queen, just like her mother, was bad at that.' She could compartmentalise things so they just went away – only they didn't.

In many ways, Philip was somewhat the opposite of his wife, being outspoken on various subjects because he wasn't bound by the rules of impartiality. He was always forthright in expressing himself, even on occasions when his own actions might have appeared contrary to his stated views. In 1961, the Queen and Prince Philip embarked on a forty-four-day tour of the Indian subcontinent, including Pakistan and Nepal. One of the engagements on the tour was a visit to Jaipur at the invitation of the Maharajah, who had organised a tiger shoot as part of the entertainment for the royal couple. When asked about the shoot by reporters at a prior reception in Delhi, Philip said: 'Of course I plan to shoot a tiger if possible. Why not?' It was the same year that Philip and others were in the process of setting up the World Wildlife Fund, of which he was about to become president of the UK branch.

The shoot went ahead, with a tethered buffalo as bait for the tiger. When photographs of Philip and his party with the dead tigress he had shot were transmitted across the Commonwealth, there was a barrage of criticism in the foreign press, accusing Philip of cruelty to animals and of reliving the old days of the Empire. A second, more elaborate tiger shoot had been organised by the King of Nepal some weeks later. When Philip appeared in Nepal, his trigger finger was encased in a large white bandage after it had mysteriously become infected since the shooting of the tigress in India. It was left to Philip's treasurer, Sir Christopher Bonham-Carter, to shoot the tiger, thus saving Philip from further heavy criticism. Throughout his life Philip enjoyed the shoots, at Sandringham and elsewhere, in which vast numbers of birds were driven towards a line of guns, bringing them down in large numbers. He never considered the killing of wildlife to be in conflict with his position as president of the World Wildlife Fund.

As one of the world's foremost conservationists, Philip was vociferous in expressing the threats posed by humans to the natural world. He long argued that the 'greenhouse effect' and global warming are threats to the future of mankind and more than once stated that the greatest problem the world faces is what he described as 'the colossal increase in the human population . . . which is reaching plague proportions'. He felt so strongly about this that in 2008, during an interview with the German newspaper *Bild*, he made the extraordinary statement: 'In the event that I am reincarnated I would like to return as a deadly virus in order to contribute something to solve overpopulation.' Having secured an heir and a spare with his and Princess Elizabeth's first two children, there seemed little need for Philip to have two more sons. If anyone had had the temerity to question Philip on the subject, in light of his stated views on overpopulation, Philip would no doubt have taken the view that he could have as many children as he felt like.

After Princess Elizabeth acceded to the throne, Philip had to take second place in all matters of state. In public appearances he was always two steps behind the Queen. This cannot have come easily to such a forceful personality. However, when it came to domestic and family matters, Philip was very much the master of the house. He had the final decision over which schools the heir to the throne would attend, he chose the furnishing and fittings of family homes, he organised the shoots at Sandringham and any invitations for personal guests at Balmoral. Due to his interest in all things epicurean, he sometimes also chose the menus. The Queen, being averse to confrontation of any kind, would go along with whatever Philip decided, and Charles, unlike his feisty sister Anne, did not have the personality to stand up to his father.

As a child, the sensitive and shy Prince Charles was reduced to tears when upbraided by his father for some aspect of his behaviour. And it was not only when correcting Charles that Philip brought tears to his son's eyes – he would often belittle him in front of guests. In his biography of Charles, Jonathan Dimbleby quotes a close relation of Charles who was on good terms with both Prince Philip and Prince Charles, and who referred to the rough and bullying way in which the father addressed his son in public, which had the effect of driving Charles more and more back into his shell. In an interview with Cliff Michelmore for BBC television in 1969, when asked if his father was a tough disciplinarian and whether Charles had ever been told to sit down and shut up, Prince Charles answered: 'The whole time, yes! I think he had quite a strong influence on me, particularly in my younger days.'

Philip has come under some criticism for sending his shy and sensitive son to boarding school at Cheam and then at Gordonstoun. In doing so, he was only following a long English aristocratic tradition that sons should follow their fathers when it came to schooling. Philip himself went to Cheam because he was following in the footsteps of George Milford Haven, who was acting *in loco parentis* while Philip's father was in France. Philip's older sister Theodora decided to take him out of Cheam and enrol him at Schule Schloss Salem in Germany, which had the added advantage of freeing Philip's family from paying school fees. Kurt Hahn, Salem's founder, was a brilliant educator who had an enormous influence on Philip. When he had to flee Germany due to Nazi persecution, Hahn founded Gordonstoun school in Scotland, and Philip became one of its earliest pupils. Philip had the greatest respect for Hahn, who later was instrumental in setting up the Duke of Edinburgh's Award scheme.

During his time at Gordonstoun, Prince Charles took two terms off to attend Geelong Grammar School's Timbertop campus in the Australian outback. He would later tell his penfriend Rosaleen Bagge that he was very

. happy in Australia, perhaps happier there than he had ever been in his life. Finally, Prince Philip had done the right thing by his son; Philip claimed it was his idea that Charles should go to Australia and he assigned his equerry, Sir David Checketts, to accompany Charles in the unofficial role of private secretary and advisor. The idea was in fact the result of a committee presided over by the Queen, but she allowed Philip to make the final decision, as she knew nothing about schooling, having been educated only by various governesses. Charles had accepted the idea with alacrity, even though the school was in the wilds near Mansfield in Victoria and had the reputation of being pretty tough.

The idea that Philip or the Queen had much knowledge of what went on during their eldest son's education is doubtful because Charles never confided the extent of his unhappiness to his abrasive father or his busy mother. Rather than sympathising with his son's subdued state of mind, Philip dutifully wrote to him encouraging him to 'man up' and learn to be strong and resourceful.

The educational experiment planned by his father eventually came to its conclusion. But what had been achieved, and at what cost? Charles had learned how to keep his emotions in check, how always to present a brave face, but the little boy who cowered when his father raised his voice still lurked under the surface.

There was no way his father could turn Charles into the man he wanted him to be, in spite of putting him through the refined hardship of Cheam, Gordonstoun and

Timbertop. There was no way, either, that Philip was going to admit that his insistence on sending him to Gordonstoun was a mistake, or that Charles was going to step down from his stance that he had been 'emotionally estranged' from his parents, who had been 'unable or unwilling' to offer the kind of affection he craved.

In 1965, when the Queen and the Duke of Edinburgh set up a committee at Buckingham Palace to discuss Charles's future education, it was eventually decided that he should first go to Cambridge and then join the Royal Navy. It was the Dean of Windsor who chose Trinity College specifically. Cambridge had the advantage of being relatively near to Sandringham, where Charles had become accustomed to joining the guns during the shooting season, and it became his habit during the season to invite his university friends to take part in the shoot and joining him for the weekend at Wood Farm on the Sandringham estate.

The Queen made a private visit to Trinity College to view Charles's living quarters, after which his rooms were redecorated. Charles achieved a second-class degree for his studies in Archaeology, Anthropology and History. Much to his delight, his achievement was widely reported in the national press. He wrote to David Checketts: 'I am so pleased that the papers have given the exam results a fit deal. I have achieved my desire anyway and shown them in some small way at least that I am not totally ignorant or incompetent. The tables will now be turned and I will be envisaged as a princely swot!' Indeed, during his second year at Cambridge he spent a term at the University College of Wales, where he had to get his head down and learn the rudiments of the Welsh language in preparation for his investiture as Prince of Wales.

By 1971, when Prince Charles began his five-year stint in the Royal Navy, having first earned his wings on jet planes at RAF Cranwell, he had developed a degree of self-confidence that had previously been lacking. Far from being shy and retiring, he was well on the way to becoming the 'Action Man' that the press was to dub him. He was a fearless rider in the hunting field and playing polo had become a passion – he practised for hours on a wooden horse until he was proficient enough to get a decent handicap of three. Skiing was another sport he took up, staying with his friends the Palmer-Tomkinsons in Klosters, Switzerland. A stay at this resort became an annual fixture.

In the meantime, Prince Philip had played a major part in a project that was to involve the whole family. It was considered one of the very few errors of judgement that Philip made in his endeavours to support the monarchy. In 1968, an opportunity arose that suited Philip's ideas for popularising and modernising the monarchy through the medium of television. During a weekend at the Norfolk home of Lord Buxton, Philip was approached by Dickie Mountbatten's son-in-law, Lord Brabourne, with the idea of making a behind-the-scenes television documentary about the royal family. Philip liked the idea since he knew there was 'nothing between the court circular and the gossip columns' and felt it was time for the monarchy to meet the medium of television on its own terms. When the discussions became serious, he insisted the Queen should be consulted before it went any further. Surprisingly, she was not averse to the idea, on one condition, to which the BBC had to agree: if she didn't like the film, the entire thing would be canned.

Richard Cawston, head of the documentary department of the BBC, was suggested as director, and it was agreed the BBC were to be allowed to spend a year recording the activities of the family at home and abroad, including recording unrehearsed conversations. 'It wasn't a soap', Brabourne said. 'It was a matter of portraying these people as human beings.' To an extent it did, and in the rare moments the Queen seemed to be at ease, it showed her as quick and humorous. Philip appeared energetic and impatient but kind and Charles an awkward but dutiful older brother. Prince Philip liked the result. He believed the film helped pave the way to people's understanding that the monarchy was a workday business and its figurehead was just doing a job. 'I think it is quite wrong that there should be a sense of remoteness about majesty,' Philip said when asked about the film. 'If people see whoever it happens to be, whatever head of state, as individuals, as people, I think it makes it much easier for them to accept the system or to feel part of the system.'

The film had its critics and many to this day believe it 'started the rot' by offering an intimacy never previously provided, leaving the public and the press hungry for more. Some even said the film encouraged the discarding of any remaining restraint. 'The sight of Prince Philip cooking sausages meant that after that people would want to see the dining room, the sitting room and everything except the loo,' said the eminent historian Kenneth Rose, who subscribed to the 'started the rot' theory. It was thought that by portraying the royals as an ordinary family, the mystique surrounding them had been destroyed. Philip's opinion, however, was that if it hadn't happened, then it would have been even more difficult to control the monarchy's image in the future. In any event, they could hardly be considered by viewers of the documentary as an ordinary family, living as they were in a series of palaces and being waited upon by an army of servants.

In 1976, Prince Charles set up the Prince's Trust with the aim of helping vulnerable young people from the UK and the Commonwealth, the latter part of which especially pleased his mother. In his desire to help young people, Charles was also following in his father's footsteps. The Duke of Edinburgh's Award scheme was already well established and was giving many thousands of young people the opportunity to achieve personal development through sports, volunteering and completing courses to gain the awards. While different in their modus operandi, both the Prince's Trust and the Duke's Award scheme aimed to help young people get on in the world. In setting up the Trust, Prince Charles had been showing his father that he too could achieve something worthwhile. Although he had been surrounded by sycophants all his life and had the love of his nannies and governess, he was deprived of crucial nurturing by the two people that really mattered, his mother and his father, and even in adulthood he was always trying to find ways of winning their approval.

Charles and his father were so totally opposite that they never completely trusted one another. Prince Philip was brought up in a world run almost entirely by men and Charles was brought up in a world run almost entirely by women. Charles was forever trying to please his father, but had a perverse knack of doing exactly the opposite. On the polo field, Philip would be particularly brutal to Charles when they played together, and polo player Johnny Kidd, father of supermodel Jodie, remembers Philip screaming abuse at his son when he made some minor mistake or missed a shot. Admittedly, Philip shouted at everyone, but it was particularly embarrassing for the other players to hear him rant and rave at his son.

Nonetheless, after his father died, Charles spoke warmly of his 'dear Papa', a 'very special person who . . . above all else would have been amazed by the reaction and the touching things that have been said about him'. He continued: 'His energy was astonishing, in supporting my mama, and doing it for such a long time, and in some extraordinary way being able to go on doing it for so long. What he has done has amounted to an astonishing achievement.' Meanwhile, Prince Andrew told the BBC he would remember his father as one who would come home in the evening and 'read to us, like in any other family'.

Two brothers with disparate memories of their father –

one recalling the loving warmth of him reading bedtime stories, the other full of admiration for his father's unfailing support of his mother for seventy years. With Charles, Philip had allowed his feelings of frustration to show; with Andrew, they had only manifested when he had failed to live up to his father's early hopes for a promising career.

Both sons were a disappointment to Philip. Neither of them wanted to emulate their father in personality, although they were full of admiration for what he had done for their mother and the institution of the monarchy, which he fought so hard to support.

Quality love – the presence of continuing availability – was never there for Charles from his father, so he learned to do without him. Even on the day of Prince Philip's funeral at St George's Chapel, Windsor Castle, as recounted in the Duke of Sussex's memoir *Spare*, Charles appeared unconcerned. He had left his father's wake to try to be a father himself to Princes William and Harry; he hoped to broker a deal between his warring sons. Instead, the three of them made small talk about the funeral they had just attended. They agreed it was pleasing to know that Prince Philip had planned it all himself down to the tiniest detail. Harry had previously spoken to his grandfather about death and Philip had explained to him that although he was no longer capable of 'pursuing his passions', the one thing he missed most was work. '"Without work,"' he said to Harry, '"everything crumbles."' Harry explains that his grandfather didn't seem sad, just ready. '"You have to know when it's time to go, Harry,"' he told him.

Prince Charles had been at Highgrove when he received the news his father had died peacefully in the early morning of 9 April at Windsor Castle. The Duke had a hospital bed set up in his dressing room and a small team of nurses supervising him around the clock. That morning, they were helping him to the shower, when he told them he felt unwell and dizzy. Having got him back into bed, one of the nurses immediately called the Duke's valet and the Queen's page, Paul Whybrew. But it was too late – the Duke had died almost immediately and before the Queen could reach his bedside. The Prince of Wales arrived at the castle as his father was being laid out by the doctor, but didn't stay to see him, returning later in the afternoon to pay his last respects. It was his wedding anniversary – sixteen years previously he had been at Windsor preparing for his marriage to Camilla Parker Bowles.

Perhaps the only thing Charles and both his parents had in common – although it manifested itself in different ways – was that they were all believers. King Charles is more spiritual; the Queen was a believer in true Christian values and said her prayers every night, while Prince Philip questioned everything but still believed in God.

The former Archbishop of York John Sentamu recalled speaking to Prince Philip about his faith. 'Our Queen and I are so strong in our belief in Christ,' Philip told the Archbishop, before they shared a moment of prayer for the Duke's children, whose complicated marriages were troubling him at the time.

Unfortunately, Prince Philip was never able to communicate with Charles in the way he was able to with God. The lines of communication between them were far too tenuous and they were not used to speaking about their feelings until it was too late. Charles loved his father, but I am not sure he ever liked him.

9

DIANA

Lady Diana Spencer enjoyed telling people that she had met her future husband when she was still wearing nappies. 'I've known him all my life,' she'd announce. Those nappy days, and the years that followed, were spent in Norfolk at Park House, a ten-bedroom Victorian mansion on the edge of the Queen's Sandringham estate. It was not grand by royal standards, but there were six staff, including a full-time cook. Built by Edward VII to accommodate the overflow of shooting guests from Sandringham House, it had come into the family through Diana's grandfather, Lord Fermoy, who had rented the property from George V.

Shortly after Diana's mother Frances married the 7th Earl Spencer's heir, Viscount Althorp, Lord Fermoy died, and the newlyweds took over the lease. And it was here, late in the evening of 1 July 1961, that Diana Frances Spencer was born and the course of royal history was changed.

When the Queen discovered that her son and heir was 'courting' the young Lady Diana Spencer, she was delighted.

'She is one of us,' she said. And in the roundabout way the aristocracy liked to operate, she was. The Spencers and the royal family were old allies. Diana's paternal grand-mother, Cynthia, daughter of the Duke of Abercorn, had been courted by the Prince of Wales (before he abdicated to become the Duke of Windsor), before marrying the 7th Earl Spencer in 1919.

When they weren't being romanced by the royal family, the Spencers were usually to be found serving it and being honoured in return. Edward VII was godfather to Diana's grandfather, and his wife Cynthia was the late Queen Mother's Lady of the Bedchamber. Diana's father, Johnnie, was equerry to King George VI and later to his daughter, the new Queen, whose sister, Princess Margaret, he once dated.

On Diana's maternal side, her family were also closely linked with the throne. Her mother's father, Lord Fermoy, was a shooting and tennis-playing friend of George VI. His redoubtable wife, Ruth, who would play such an encour-aging role during Diana's courtship, was the Queen Mother's Woman of the Bedchamber and one of her close friends. It was an association that prompted the description of the Spencers as royal groupies, but it also bestowed in Diana an all-important natural ease in the presence of the royal family. She was proud of her aristocratic background. It gave her a sense of belonging and she felt she was some-body, even if she wasn't very bright or intellectual. Later in her life she turned completely against her background and shied away from anything that smacked of the aristocracy. But as a teenager it enabled her to hold her own with any kind of company.

Janet Thompson, who was Diana's nanny for two and a half years, recalled one particular tea party at Sandringham House in the mid-1960s, when five-year-old Diana was playing with six-year-old Prince Andrew. Thompson remembered walking into the drawing room after hearing a voice calling out 'Where are you?', only to discover it was the Queen and she was playing hide-and-seek with the two children. 'It was all so normal, really,' Thompson said. 'It wasn't the Queen playing with the children, just a mother having fun with them. It was a lovely sight.'

Diana remembers seeing Prince Charles for the first time at another tea party, when the teenage Prince came into the nursery after a day's shooting to see what all the noise was about – little Prince Edward had just covered his face with honey and was squealing with delight. 'There was a lot of noise going on,' Thompson recalled. 'I remember Charles called out: "Is everything alright? It looks like a good party to me."'

Renowned for his easy charm, Diana's father Johnnie Spencer had been equerry to the Queen's father George VI and quickly became a firm favourite among the family. When the King died, in 1952, it seemed natural for Johnnie to carry on as equerry to his daughter Elizabeth II, which he did for two more years. The royal connection was further strengthened by the fact that Diana's eldest sister, Sarah, was a goddaughter of the Queen Mother, and her middle sister, Lady Jane Fellowes, has the Duke of Kent as a godparent. Diana's brother Charles, now 9th Earl Spencer, is also a godson of the late Queen.

The Queen only really got to know her son's girlfriends if the romance coincided with the extended Balmoral break and they could be invited to stay as part of the house party. Some were more popular than others – in particular, Lady Jane Wellesley. In many ways theirs would have been an ideal match; certainly, the Queen thought so. Self-confident in a relaxed, unstuffy way, Jane fitted in well, getting up early in the morning to see the guns off for their day's shooting, joining the Queen for a ride later in the morning, always cheerful and helpful. 'The Queen was very fond of her,' a member of the royal household recalled. Jane Wellesley had one flaw, however. She was too intelligent. Having worked in public relations, she went on to make a career for herself in broadcasting, which brought her into close contact with media intellectuals. She could see what restrictions and demands would be placed upon her if she agreed to marry Charles and the idea did not appeal to her. 'I couldn't, just couldn't give everything up to become his wife,' she said. Altogether, her romance with the Prince lasted some eighteen months, but their friendship survived the experience and she remained on his reserve list for years afterwards. Charles knew that, should a girl drop out of an opera attendance or some other engagement at the last moment (something that happened more frequently than he liked to admit), he could telephone Jane, secure in the knowledge that she would not take offence at the lateness of the call, and ask her to make up the numbers – which, if she was free, she was happy to do.

Amanda Knatchbull was another of the Queen's favourites. Easy-going and undemanding, theirs was the kind of relationship Charles was able to understand. She was also Lord Mountbatten's granddaughter and Charles's second cousin. With Mountbatten having married his nephew Philip to the future Queen, it would have been the fulfilment of his all-consuming dynastic ambitions to have married his granddaughter to the future King – and he came closer to achieving that coup than is generally known.

Amanda was, as Mountbatten pointed out, a member of the family and understood the responsibility of the job. He did everything he could to encourage the notion, and under his overpowering influence the couple began to see each other in a romantic light. Charles even proposed to her during a holiday in the Bahamas, but she ultimately regarded him as a friend and said it was not a good idea. By the summer of 1979, just after Charles had reached his self-imposed deadline of marrying before his thirtieth birthday, there was a luncheon in the Queen's private dining room at Buckingham Palace. It was attended by the Queen, Prince Philip, Lord Mountbatten, Prince Charles and Amanda Knatchbull. Members of the royal household have said they believed the final arrangements for an engagement, to be announced in early 1980, were discussed that day. At the very least, it clearly signified that the romance was well on the course upon which Mountbatten, the dynastic navigator par excellence, had set it.

Mountbatten was never called upon to bring the relationship to fruition. On 27 August 1979, while on holiday at Classiebawn Castle in County Sligo, he was blown up by the IRA. Had Mountbatten lived, many in the royal household believed that Charles would have married Amanda and the future history of the royal family would have been duller but a lot more secure. Without Mountbatten's indomitable enthusiasm to prop up the relationship, and at the same time propel it forward, it withered under the weight of mutual apathy. There simply was not the passion there to carry them through.

That had not mattered in the past. Indeed, Queen Mary would have been aghast at the suggestion that a royal marriage was anything more than a necessary and not particularly pleasant act of state. Mountbatten continued to argue that arranged marriages had a better chance of survival than those built on 'the shifting sand of love', and in that he had the support of Prince Philip, who, when appraised of his uncle's plan, remarked, 'Good. It beats having strangers coming into the family!' Amanda's parents took an altogether more modern view of how best their daughter's life might be lived. She had a right to expect more, and Charles, who had no great desire to get married, agreed. They parted on the best of terms, like brother and sister, which was how they had regarded each other before the great matchmaker had involved them in his last and grandest scheme.

In the summer of 1980, Diana Spencer went to Balmoral to stay with her sister Jane, who was married to Robert

Fellowes (later Baron Fellowes), then the Queen's assistant private secretary. After becoming the Queen's own private secretary, he would a decade later be faced with the impossible task of trying to contain the damage his sister-in-law had caused within the royal family. The Queen had given Fellowes (the son of her Sandringham land agent) the use of a cottage on the Balmoral estate, three miles along a lane from Balmoral Castle. But at that moment in time Diana was visiting just to help look after Jane's newborn daughter Laura. After a second visit to her sister, however, Diana was invited to spend four days at the castle to join one of the regular house parties.

One member of staff recalled Diana being desperate to make an impression. 'Most of the ladies do not get up until after the guns have gone out, but Diana was always up early. If you looked out of your window at a quarter to eight, you would see her walking in the garden, and she made a great point of being there to see them off.'

They continued: 'It was then that she played her sharpest card. She would go around telling everybody how much she loved Balmoral and that it was such a magical place and how she loved it beyond imagination.' Charles started asking her to accompany him fishing. He asked her to join him on long walks through the estate in which she professed such an interest. Charles was suitably impressed, as he had every reason to be, for in those early days, before illness and unhappiness took their toll, Diana, everyone agreed, was 'enchanting'.

The Queen passed no public comment and the only

reservation she had was whether one as young as Diana could differentiate between the man and the Prince. The Queen had no inkling about Diana's emotional problems at the time, but she couldn't help thinking that someone Diana's age would be far better suited to her younger son, Andrew.

The Queen Mother took a more positive approach and assured her daughter it did not matter. A month later, she invited Diana and Charles for a few days' stalking at Birkhall, her house on the Balmoral estate. It was a grand-motherly intervention and in that she had been encouraged by Diana's own grandmother, Ruth, Lady Fermoy, who was one of the Queen Mother's oldest friends. The two ladies were both very fond of the gambolling nineteen-year-old and would prove to be vital allies in the months ahead. As flirtation escalated into a rush towards marriage, Charles, who was never very sure of the wisdom of what he was doing, sought reassurance. Many of his romances had floundered when his girlfriends had decided that not even marriage to the next King was compensation enough for week after weary week every year in the rain-soaked Highlands with your mother-in-law and most of your husband's family.

Once back in London, Charles started to invite Diana out. It was discreet and low-key, but for those familiar with Charles's courtship pattern, the signs were obvious. He took her to the ballet and paid her the singular honour of inviting her to Buckingham Palace. She arrived in her Mini Metro just after 6.30 in the evening, drove through the archway into the quadrangle and was shown up in the lift to Charles's apartment on the second floor. Other girls had been up to his quarters. Indeed, only a few months earlier, his then girlfriend Anna Wallace had watched the rehearsals for the Trooping the Colour from there. But before that only Amanda Knatchbull had been given the Buckingham Palace treatment on a date, so Diana's presence there was quite enough to fuel Charles's staff's speculation.

The rumours were given further impetus when Diana was invited in November to Wood Farm on the Sandringham estate to celebrate Charles's thirty-second birthday and were confirmed when she arrived at the big house at Sandringham in January. She made a point of going into the nursery and making a great fuss of nanny Mabel Anderson, who was then looking after Princess Anne's son, Peter Phillips, but who remained the emotional lynchpin in Charles's life. And when the guns went out early in the morning, Diana was always there to wave them off with an ingratiating remark about how 'wonderful' Sandringham was. 'She was everywhere, picking up the birds, being terribly gracious and absolutely oozing charm,' a royal confidant remembered. 'And she looked marvellous, very relaxed and quite thrilled with herself.'

The same could not be said of Charles. If Diana was indeed 'home and dry', as one of his staff put it, by January, the Prince remained his usual reserved self. 'He certainly didn't look as though he had just found the most wonderful girl in the world,' a fellow guest observed. But then, that was not what Prince Charles was looking for. As he once explained, he was looking for 'someone whose interests I could share' and who could share his. 'A woman,' he continued, 'not only marries a man, she marries into a way of life, a job.' That was especially true in his case and Charles explained in great detail to Diana the demands that would be placed on her if she became his wife. They also discussed the age gap. Diana had at first been concerned by the twelve-year difference but that soon got lost in the excitement of the courtship that was rushing them both along at a speed over which they soon lost control.

Despite all of Diana's many positive attributes, any set of in-laws takes a little getting used to, and the Windsors are in a class of their own. Self-contained and wary of those to whom they are not related by blood, they only welcome people on their own terms. Diana had to adapt herself to a whole ritual of familial quirks. Some were simply foibles of a kind all families have, like the way they laid their pudding spoons and forks across the top of the place setting, in a way she had always been told was very bourgeois; how, at Balmoral, they used fish knives, which were supposed to be the height of pretentious vulgarity; and how at Christmas they all tried to outdo each other in the meanness of their presents.

There was the Queen's trick of leaving her chocolates out on the grand piano in the Saloon by the front entrance at Sandringham and then peering down unseen from the window in the corridor overhead to see who would filch one. She took delight in teasing the embarrassed culprits, who could not fathom how they had been found out. Then there was her practice of picking ticks off the corgis and flicking them into the fire, where they landed with a satisfying hiss in the flames.

It was all very confusing to someone as young, inexperienced and so fundamentally lacking in self-confidence as Diana. Of far greater concern, however, was the emotional sterility of the royal family. Even something as innocuous as a birthday is all but ignored. The royal family, for whom every week brings its share of anniversaries and dates that must be observed, make light of birthdays, unless they are decade birthdays or can be woven into something else. When Prince Andrew turned twenty-one, in February 1981, the Queen decided to combine his birthday with a traditional Ascot-week ball, which had recently been discontinued as part of the Palace's economy drive. In other words, it was an excuse for a lavish thousand-person white-tie-and-tails knees-up of the grandest kind for her favourite son.

Elton John provided the cabaret and, although he was a friend of Andrew's, he did not mingle with the other guests. Instead, he waited in an anteroom while he readied himself for his performance. Even a star of Elton's lustre was nervous about playing in front of this particular audience. Shortly after midnight, he came out onto the stage in the Waterloo Chamber, where the royals gather every year on the anniversary of Wellington's great victory over Napoleon and where, four decades before, the Queen and Princess Margaret had performed their wartime pantomimes. With all his showman's charm, he dedicated his first tune, 'Your

Song', to the Queen. 'It was a very nervy experience,' Elton later recalled in a television interview with presenter Graham Norton:

Ray Cooper, my percussion player, and myself played, and you looked over the balcony at all these gold chairs and suddenly they fill up and you think, 'Oh God . . .'. We played, and I came down and I changed, and I was in a ballroom with a band and Diana Spencer. She wasn't married to Prince Charles yet and she said, 'Do you want to dance?', and I can't dance anyway, but we did a faux Charleston and then we went into dinner. Then Princess Anne said, 'Shall we go into the disco?' and it was the quietest disco you have ever heard. And then the Queen came in and she said, 'Can we join you?' And we went straight into Bill Haley's 'Rock Around the Clock', and I thought, *This is ridiculous*. It was one of the most surreal moments of my life.

It was one of the most surreal moments of Diana's life, too. The Queen may have been having fun dancing with Elton John, but Charles was behaving as if he was on duty and insisted, to the despair of his fiancée, on working the room and making sure he spoke with as many people as possible. Joe Loss and his orchestra kept the older guests on their feet. The younger crowd congregated in the disco, where the music was louder. Diana, nervous, upset and emotionally drained, danced frantically with first one man, then another and eventually by herself. As the sun began to rise, her newfound ally and member of the royal household staff, Mark Simpson, glanced out of the window and saw Diana in the quadrangle, cutting a gaunt figure in the half-light, looking exhausted, lost in her thoughts, but still moving in a slow, rhythmic time to the music that was now playing in her head.

The police checked her out at 5.30 a.m., when she set off in her car for Althorp, her father's home in Northamptonshire. At that moment, she was distraught, flustered and had no intention of ever going back. Her wedding to Charles was mere weeks away. As far as Diana was concerned that morning, it was cancelled. In her anger and despair, she had decided she was not going through with it.

When the Queen was informed that Lady Diana had left the castle at first light that Sunday, she assumed that Charles was in on the arrangement. Never one to interfere in family affairs, she didn't think to ask her son where his fiancée was. She was aware that Diana had to struggle through the majority of Ascot week without Charles, as he was in the United States. She was also aware Diana was nervous about the forthcoming wedding – but that was it. It was always the busiest week of the Queen's year, starting with the Order of the Garter ceremony on the Monday and traditionally ending with the Ascot ball on the Saturday. For the Queen, it was church as usual, and there simply wasn't the time to be concerned about Diana.

Diana's father calmed her down and pointed out it would have been an act of gross discourtesy to break off the engagement to the future King so close to the wedding –

and wasn't it what she had always wanted? Had she not assured her father when he told her, 'You must only marry the man you love,' and she had said, 'That is what I am doing'? Earl Spencer had never fully recovered from the stroke that had almost killed him in 1978, and for the rest of his life he found it difficult to talk when he was over-excited or upset. Diana's crisis focused his mind and over the course of the weekend, between tears and indecision, he talked Diana round. She always regarded her father as very wise and listened to his advice even if she didn't take it. According to Dame Barbara Cartland, who was the mother of the Earl's second wife, Raine Spencer, 'Diana didn't know half the things she ought to have known about. My son-in-law had been equerry to the Queen, but Diana was only a little girl at the time and he didn't teach her anything. She did not know the rules and regulations. It all came as a shock to her and therefore she found it very difficult. She started off on the wrong foot.'

But Diana wanted to be Princess of Wales. She was young enough to be certain it would all be all right, and she believed in happy endings. Meanwhile, Charles had no comprehension of the compromises and concessions that go into the making of a modern marriage. He had only ever had to look out for himself, and right now he needed a wife. He was, and still is, a loner, which is why he loves spending time on his own at the Castle of Mey, his grand-mother the Queen Mother's former home in the north of Scotland. He now goes there alone every summer, to enjoy the space and seclusion he loves. It enables him to function at his own pace and go fishing. Charles needed a woman who was confident enough not to have to be constantly at his side, and Diana was never that woman, as much as she tried to be in the beginning. Later in her short life, she acknowledged that the timing was wrong but still fervently believed that, had they met at a different moment in their lives, things might have worked out between them.

Years later, when the Queen was discussing the failure of her children's marriages with her mother Queen Elizabeth, she asked: 'Where did I go wrong?' The Queen Mother, who never liked discussing anything controversial, dismissed her worries with a wave of her hand. 'It's another generation,' she answered simply. 'There is nothing you can do.'

There was, of course, a good deal that could have been done. If the Queen had been a different sort of person – someone who was better able to deal with emotional confrontation – she could have helped. But when she was not shielded by her courtiers, she was protected by her uncanny ability to change the subject when anything arose that she didn't want to confront. Her trump card was what Prince Philip called her 'dog mechanism'. This worked in a variety of different ways – as an excuse to leave the room and avoid a prickly situation or a way of diffusing a potentially awkward discussion by calling the dogs to her side and bringing them into the conversation. The Duke and Duchess of York experienced this when they were trying to talk to the Queen about their marital problems. Another time, Princess Anne and her future second husband Tim

Laurence went to talk to the former Dean of Windsor, Michael Mann, about getting married. He asked the Princess if she had spoken to her mother about it. 'You know how difficult it is to talk to the Queen about these things. Aunt Margaret always says that the only time to see her is when she is on her own and the dogs are not there – and then she's usually too tired.' It took Anne three weekends before she could nail her mother down for the conversation. Years later, Harry says he was also prevented from talking to his grandmother. Having agreed a meeting with her on the phone, he was later told she was too busy to see him and that she had made a mistake over timings. The Queen had spent her whole life adhering to timetables and had never been late or missed an appointment. It was an excuse, and he knew it.

Diana was the only one who dared to interrupt the Queen – a monarch who exuded what can best be called true 'majesty'. Indeed, when her staff went to see her, they talked about going into her 'presence', which was an apt description, for in her presence even diehard republicans found themselves tongue-tied by deference. Diana, however, had no fear and would wait in the page's vestibule next to the Queen's private rooms, often in tears and full of tales of woe, and as soon as the Queen's visitor had departed, would ensure she was ushered into the room almost before the page had had time to announce her. Once she was there, Diana would run through her stock of grievances and let all her emotions out. She railed against her mother, her stepmother, her sister Sarah McCorquodale, her husband and anyone else who had upset her. She insisted no one understood her, that everyone else was to blame, that she was being victimised. For the Queen, who had never had to deal with these kinds of outbursts in her life, it was bewildering, and she was emotionally caught off-balance.

The Queen kept a careful note of these encounters. She prided herself on her excellent memory; even in her later years, she could recall a date or an event precisely. She took a careful mental note of Diana's objections, which came to be replaced by more strident protests. Diana's brother-in-law, Robert Fellowes, then the Queen's assistant private secretary, was a particular target. Diana had demonised him in her imagination and she described him as a pompous bully. Fellowes did his best when ministering to his sister-in-law but he was in a very difficult situation. The Queen understood this, but although court protocol meant Fellowes had to take the lead from her, she was reluctant to make any decision. 'She just procrastinated,' a member of the royal household said at the time. She listened to what Diana said, 'but no solution was ever put forward.'

The Queen came to dread the meetings with her daughter-in-law. They left her feeling drained, despondent and confused – an uncommon state for a woman accustomed to the certainties of her position. The problems were there from the beginning, but no one saw them apart from Charles, and he was not going to tell his mother he had made a mistake; they had never had that kind of relationship. The royal family never discussed their personal problems with each other and, as Charles's official biographer, Jonathan Dimbleby, noted, 'For the Prince's part, the prospect of discussing such problems with his parents was almost inconceivable. Yet, incapable as they were of reaching out to each other, all three understood only too well the overriding rule of royal life: the show goes on.'

As is frequently the case in royal households, the only people who were aware of what was really going on were the staff. One, Prince Edward's footman Mark Simpson, became particularly close to Diana. Due to his youth and sensitivity, the consensus was that he would be the right member of staff to help Diana through her early Buckingham Palace days, and they became friends.

On more than one occasion, their friendship came under fire, however – the first time being when the Prince came back from America and was driven straight to Windsor Castle, as it was Royal Ascot week. Simpson recalled: 'Lady Diana ran down to the private entrance to greet him as he got out of the car, and he gave her a peck on the cheek and walked straight inside. I was walking down the corridor past the Shelter Rooms, where Diana was staying, and she called me into her sitting room.' He continued: 'I went in, and she broke down in floods of tears and just sobbed and sobbed for at least half an hour.' Simpson felt the Princess needed a hug. 'I felt so sorry for her – and then Lady Susan Hussey [the Queen's lady in waiting] came in while I had my arms around her. That was a big mistake – for me, anyway. She was fine with me, but she didn't think the future Princess of Wales should have her arms around a footman. She came in and went straight out. I was mortified, but what could I do?'

After the engagement, she wasn't at the palace very much and it wasn't until May, June and July of 1981 that I started seeing her every day and we had these great long chats. She told me she hated the engagement photos and she thought she looked fat, which was when her bulimia started. We talked about everything. She said how unfeeling the family was; how they had no emotion and Prince Charles wasn't paying her any attention, and there was a great long list of people she hated and loathed. She hated Lady Susan Hussey, and she hated Princess Anne. She told me her mother was a ruthless woman and a self-promoter, but I knew it was just a phase, as she would go shopping with her mother the following morning and her mother helped her a lot.

She even claimed the Queen wasn't paying her any attention. To be fair, Buckingham Palace is a workplace; it's not somewhere where the Queen has got endless hours to spare having cosy chats with Lady Diana over lunch. And of course, Prince Charles's work schedule had already been planned before the engagement. I tried to explain to her as much as I could about the royal family. I said they are not terrible people, but they are very busy and they don't get involved in situations as they don't have time for them. I think Diana thought it was strange that the Queen was not up there with her, sitting on the end of her bed chatting to her about her day. I think she genuinely thought that was going to happen.

When the Queen is at the palace, any of her children – and at that stage that included Diana Spencer – are welcome to have any meal they want with Her Majesty and all they have to do is phone up the Queen's page and say, 'Is the Queen in for lunch today and if so, does she have anybody with her? And would it be all right if I came down?' And then the page would say, 'She's got an appointment and no, it wouldn't be okay; or else she is on her own and it would be perfectly fine.' The Queen loved it if her children had lunch with her or dinner as she was often on her own. She would be as flexible as she could if she thought her children could join her. She loved it. I felt it was my job to explain to Diana that if she wanted to eat with the Queen or see the Queen, all she had to do was ring up the Queen's page and find out.

And she never did. There was more:

At the time, Prince Charles wasn't making any great romantic advances towards her and I suppose the rejection was getting more acute, and she was becoming more and more unhappy. I wasn't the right person to deal with it because I didn't understand. I was a product of the palace so the more reticent approach that Prince Charles was used to was what I understood. It didn't seem strange to me that Prince Charles was out most of the time and not spending every night having dinner with her. I understood that the royal family had a huge schedule that made family life almost impossible, unless they were at Balmoral or Sandringham.

Even at Balmoral, there was never much affection shown between the various family members and if things went wrong in their lives, they were always full of bravado. From their earliest days, they are surrounded by people who are terribly nice to them and if things go wrong, it is always someone else's fault. They are used to people doing exactly what they want, so they don't expect to be told not to do something. They could all therefore be terribly arrogant, selfish and spoiled.

This was the world Diana walked into at the age of nineteen. It rubbed off on her, bringing out the worst of her insecurities and making her manipulative. She was used to getting her own way and tried to exert control over her husband in any way she could, on one occasion prostrating herself on the gravel drive begging him not to leave her as he drove off on an official engagement. In the beginning, he pandered to her and allowed her to scream and shout when she didn't get her own way or was frustrated by her life. He felt responsible for her unhappiness but was incapable of doing anything about it.

Like many mothers, even those with few maternal instincts, after her initial delight of Diana becoming 'one of us', the Queen had misgivings about the marriage but said nothing to her son. She always found a way to forgive

Diana, blaming it on her youth and hoping things would repair themselves.

On 20 November 1995, the night Diana's interview with Martin Bashir on the BBC's *Panorama* programme aired on television, the Queen and Prince Philip were at the *Royal Variety Performance*. It was also their wedding anniversary. The Queen saw the programme as a carefully prepared onslaught on the integrity of the royal family. She didn't believe for one moment it wasn't carefully rehearsed – lines such as 'There were three of us in this marriage' and 'Queen of hearts' came out too glibly. And the arresting remark 'There's no better way to dismantle a personality than to isolate it' was not off the cuff but a quote from the former Beirut hostage Brian Keenan's book *An Evil Cradling*. It was not the cries of anguish that so upset the Queen – she had been listening to those for the better part of three years. Nor was it Diana's demand that she be allotted a more positive role within the royal family that she had removed herself from. The Queen had long been an admirer of Diana's ability to empathise with the sick and needy. What was inexcusable and unforgivable was the way Diana questioned the wisdom of allowing her estranged husband – the Queen's son and heir – to ascend the throne.

Despite her own considerable doubts about her eldest son over the years, the Queen found Diana's comments more than she would tolerate. In a desperate cry of defiance, the Princess reverted to the third person and declared: 'She won't go quietly. I'll fight to the end because I believe I have a role to fulfil, and I've got two children to bring up.'

This made up the Queen's mind. It was as Head of State, rather than the hitherto accommodating mother-in-law, that the Queen finally decided to act. Early in December she wrote two letters, one hand-delivered to Diana at Kensington Palace, the other to Charles at Highgrove. In it she expressed her anger and frustration, and she spelled out her 'desire for an early divorce'.

Years later, when it was discovered that Martin Bashir had lied to Diana's brother and used forged documents and misleading information to help obtain the interview, Diana's memory was redeemed, but she still said the things that hastened her divorce. On 28 August 1996, Charles and Diana's marriage was finally annulled. The fairy tale that had turned into a nightmare was almost at its end. Diana, Princess of Wales, had only one year and three days left to live.

The death of Diana on 31 August 1997 united mother and son in shock and grief as they took control of the tragedy. Holidaying at Balmoral, they had no inkling of the crisis that would overwhelm them when they received news of her death in the early hours of that Sunday morning. The Queen's suite of rooms on the first floor of the castle were adjacent to Prince Charles's, but more than the thick walls divided them. The Queen had steadfastly refused to acknowledge Mrs Parker Bowles, and that day Charles had planned to fly south to deliver the boys to their mother before the end of the school holidays, then return to Highgrove and Camilla before heading for Provence.

Instead, he was huddled with the Queen in her sitting room, discussing what to do in between the dozens of crisis phone calls.

Charles's immediate concern was what to do about the boys. He and the Queen both agreed it would be better to let them sleep until the morning before breaking the awful news to them. Charles was also adamant he would be the one to fly to Paris and collect Diana's body. The Queen was against the idea, as Diana was no longer a member of the royal family and she felt it was wrong to make too much fuss. After much discussion, it is said that Robin Janvrin, the deputy private secretary on duty, sarcastically suggested that if they didn't do something themselves, the Princess might come back in a Harrods van. Dispatching a BAe 146 from RAF Northolt was quickly considered the best plan, despite Her Majesty's original objection. The plane picked up Diana's sisters, Lady Sarah McCorquodale and Lady Jane Fellowes, from RAF Wittering in Rutland, then flew on to Aberdeen, where they picked up the Prince and headed for Paris.

When Charles returned to Balmoral, arrangements were already being set in motion for the funeral, and once again mother and son disagreed. The Queen and the Spencers wanted a small, private, family funeral; the Queen initially thought of Frogmore as the best place, for the sake of the boys. Charles, on the other hand, felt strongly that Diana should have a full royal funeral at Westminster Abbey. There were more disagreements about who should sit on the funeral committee. Prince Charles wanted the government represented and the Queen didn't. Then there was the absence of a flag flying at half-mast over Buckingham Palace. A stickler for tradition, the Queen refused. The Royal Standard had not flown at half-mast over the palace for her father King George VI and it was not going to do so now. Nor was it going to be replaced by a Union flag.

According to royal biographer Penny Junor, it was left to Prince Charles's private secretary, Stephen Lamport, to persuade the Prince to speak to his mother about the flag: 'You've got to make her understand. You're the only person who can do it.'

Charles could not handle the Diana phenomenon and neither could his mother. They had tried to come to terms with Diana's extraordinary rapport with the British people, but they never succeeded. The royal family misjudged how the public would respond to her death, because they closed ranks, as they always had done in the past. This time it was different, and it didn't work. By remaining in Scotland, at Balmoral, when the country wanted the monarch in London with them, it created a brief but serious wobble.

The Queen was bemused by the whole scenario and couldn't understand the nation's grief for someone they didn't know, acting like one of their own family had died. She was also very alarmed at the crowd's resentment towards her outside Buckingham Palace and didn't know what people wanted her to do. She had never been able to express her emotions, especially in public, and all she did was behave as she had always behaved.

When Charles Spencer gave his remarkable funeral

address in Westminster Abbey, the Prince of Wales was extremely apprehensive. He had asked Spencer to let him see the speech beforehand and Spencer had, unsurprisingly, point-blank refused. The Prince had also found the walk behind Diana's coffin to the Abbey extremely nerve-wracking, as he had convinced himself that someone was going to take a shot at him in revenge for her death; in the silence, he could clearly hear the disparaging comments of the crowd as he walked past. According to royal biographer Robert Hardman, the night before the funeral he had tele-phoned some of his close friends, calmly acknowledging this might be their last conversation with him.

Spencer's address was seen as a message to the royal family, criticising the Queen for having stripped Diana of her title as a Royal Highness and stressing that her 'blood family' would assume guidance of the two young Princes, 'so that their souls are not simply immersed by duty and tradition, but can sing openly as you planned.' Thus implying that neither their father nor the Queen were good enough.

10

My Darling Wife, Camilla

It all began in the early '70s in an unimposing block of post-war flats in Belgravia's Ebury Street. There, 24-year-old Camilla Shand was invited by Lucía Santa Cruz, who lived in the flat above, to join her for a drink and meet the Prince of Wales, who was coming round to take her out.

The unsophisticated 22-year-old Prince can't have been a patch on Camilla's mischievous on/off boyfriend, Andrew Parker Bowles, but there was an instant warmth between the two. Lucía admitted she didn't know why she put them together – there was no rational reason except she knew that Andrew had dated Prince Charles's sister, Anne, on one of his frequent breaks from Camilla.

The idea of Charles and Camilla becoming friends, or even something more, while Andrew romanced the Prince's sister was highly amusing to both girls, especially as Camilla's great-grandmother, Alice Keppel, had been Edward VII's mistress. Alice's daughter Sonia married wealthy architect Roland Cubitt, whose grandfather Thomas was the renowned builder. By the time Sonia gave birth to Rosalind, Camilla's mother, Camilla could claim that her great-great-grandfather had been responsible for building Belgravia, Pimlico and much of the Grosvenor estate, including, for good measure, the east front of Buckingham Palace, which was designed by Edward Blore.

As the friendship turned into romance, Charles confided in his uncle, Lord Mountbatten, who told the Prince he could use his family home, Broadlands in Hampshire, whenever he wanted, so he could be alone with Camilla without anyone knowing. He never imagined for one moment that she would be the woman Charles would love for the rest of his life. Dickie Mountbatten's strict views on who Charles should marry did not at that time include Camilla Shand. He knew she would be unacceptable to the Queen, as the woman who married the heir to the throne had to have an unsullied past and come from an aristocratic background. Back in the '70s and '80s, anything else was out of the question.

The easy-going relationship between Camilla and Charles, which was conducted between London and Broadlands, came to its inevitable end at the beginning of 1973. Prince Charles's naval career demanded that he sail to the Caribbean on the frigate HMS *Minerva*, which would separate the couple for almost a year. Lovestruck Charles invited Camilla for a final weekend at Broadlands and later wrote movingly to Mountbatten, telling him it was 'the last time I shall see her for eight months'. The idea of proposing to Camilla that weekend occurred to him, but he was fearful of being rejected and failed to say anything.

With Charles out of the way, Andrew Parker Bowles and Camilla resumed their affair, and Andrew finally proposed. Naturally she accepted. She knew she could never marry the Prince of Wales, and even if she could, part of her would always love Andrew. When Charles heard the news, he was heartbroken. The unworldly Prince couldn't understand how after 'such a blissful, peaceful and mutually happy relationship', Camilla was to be taken away from him by a man who treated her so badly. 'I suppose the feeling of emptiness will pass eventually,' he wrote to a friend.

It was not a good time emotionally for Charles, as just over a month later, he received a letter from Prince Philip telling him that his sister Princess Anne was to marry an Army captain called Mark Phillips. The news gave him a 'spasm of shock and amazement' and an overwhelming sense of loss and insecurity. He convinced himself the marriage would be a ghastly mismatch. Anne had been a huge part of his life since he was two years old and now she was to belong to another world with another person. He felt miserable at the idea. He knew his mother would not understand, even if he were to attempt to confide in her, and there was no comforting presence of Camilla in his life any more. Years later, he explained to his biographer Jonathan Dimbleby that 'the family unit seemed on the point of disintegration with a newcomer barging into their private domain.'

It was an over-reaction on Charles's part, proving that although he was a young man, he still experienced the baffled hurt of a small, neglected child, so fierce was his resentment. In this one small instance, we glimpse an entirely different side of Charles, a modest insight into the complicated emotional person. Charles's emotional weakness baffled both his parents, especially the Queen, who worried about just how well he was going to be able to cope with the pressures of his life.

He would eventually learn to manage those pressures through hard work, his strong religious beliefs and the support of the woman he made his second wife, Camilla.

The Queen had known Camilla since she was in her early twenties. Andrew Parker Bowles's father, Derek, was one of the Queen Mother's closest friends, and through their friendship the then fourteen-year-old Andrew was selected to be a page at the Queen's coronation in 1953. When Derek, who was by then High Sheriff of Berkshire, died at the relatively young age of sixty-two in 1977, the Queen Mother invited Andrew and his wife Camilla to join her annual Scottish house party at Birkhall – that way, she joked, she could always keep up her tradition of having a Parker Bowles in 'residence'.

The Queen Mother was fond of Andrew and they shared a love of National Hunt racing. Andrew was a former amateur jockey and once even competed in the Grand National on his own horse. He was also Chairman of Sandown Park racecourse and a steward at Cheltenham and Newbury. He would duly escort the Queen Mother to Sandown and the Cheltenham Festival every year and she would invite him to stay with her at Royal Lodge at

Windsor – and, of course, Camilla went too. Camilla discovered she had many things in common with the last Queen Empress, besides a love of horses. They were both fanatical about gardens; Camilla herself loved the hard work of tending, designing and creating a garden.

But the closeness Camilla once shared with the Queen Mother, and to some extent her daughter the Queen, did not survive once the Queen became aware of Camilla's reintroduction to Charles's life.

'Some time in 1973,' the Queen's private secretary Lord Charteris told journalist Graham Turner when speaking to him about the Queen, 'I let her know that Charles was sleeping with Camilla Parker Bowles and that the Brigade of Guards did not like it. She made no comment, and her face didn't change in any way. What advice did she give Charles as a result of that? None at all, I should think. Yet, if she'd taken a stronger line at that point, things might have been totally different twenty years later.'

The Queen failed to take any action, but although she would not have been happy about it, she would have thought it perfectly safe as Camilla was a married woman and the affair would almost certainly run its course. The Queen did, however, make sure her senior courtiers knew never to include Mrs Parker Bowles on the guest list for any formal event, especially one where she herself might be present.

Camilla's close friend Lucía Santa Cruz, who had made the initial introduction between Charles and Camilla, believes that the late Queen's slighting of Camilla in the early days was not about Camilla as a person but more about her concern for the monarchy and the possibility that her son and heir might want to marry a divorcee, something that brought back unwelcome memories of the Duke of Windsor and Wallis Simpson. The Queen and Prince Philip disliked any whiff of scandal that might damage the monarchy, and the 'War of the Waleses' – as Diana and Charles's tempestuous marriage was named – was made even worse by the ever-present shadow of Camilla. 'When Camilla was married to Andrew Parker Bowles, she used to go to Balmoral with him and join the royal family. They got on marvellously well with her . . . But when the marriage failed and she was with Prince Charles, she was rejected and got all the blame, which was so unfair,' Lucía said.

Twenty years later, on her seventieth birthday in 2017, Camilla the Duchess of Cornwall revealed in an interview with the *Daily Mail* how difficult her life had been during those early years with Charles, when the press attention had been at its most hostile and there was little or no support from the royal family.

Camilla explained that for a year she was housebound in order to avoid the press. She said: 'I couldn't really go anywhere. But the children came and went as normal – they just got on with it – and so did great friends. It was horrid. It was a deeply unpleasant time, and I wouldn't want to put my worst enemy through it.'

In the version of events put about by Princess Diana's allies in the dying days of her and Charles's marriage, Charles had fallen straight out of the honeymoon bed into the arms of Camilla Parker Bowles. By then the timescales were being shifted for maximum effect. In a later report, he was supposed to have remained faithful for only the first two years of his marriage, while in the first account he managed to make it through to 1987 before embarking on his extramarital detour.

There was more than mere creativity to the dispute over the timing. If Charles had been seeing Camilla during his courtship of Diana and throughout their marriage, then he could have been fairly depicted as a heartless, immoral blackguard who drove a young girl to the brink of suicide. But if he had behaved in an honourable fashion for the first years of his marriage, then Diana had to shoulder a greater share of the responsibility for her own and her husband's subsequent misery. The Queen, who kept a concerned if discreet eye on the situation, had little doubt as to what the true situation was. Camilla, she said, was 'a much-maligned woman'.

Camilla appeared like a rock of sanity amid the storm of hysteria in which Charles found himself. Despite his wife's injunction against Camilla's presence, he kept in touch with her and the two continued to meet on the hunting field and periodically at dinner parties in the houses of friends. Camilla's own marriage, meanwhile, had cooled significantly after the birth of her two children and her husband's continual philandering, so she, too, was in a position to resume her friendship with Charles.

Camilla was his only hope for a bit of enjoyable 'quality life'. She gave him support and encouragement. She would

tell him, 'I am so proud of you,' and when he demurred
and said he was not worthy of such support, she would
reply, 'As usual you're underestimating yourself.'

It was a flattery and affection of a kind he had craved all
his life, coupled with a loving intimacy he had never enjoyed
with Diana. The depth of their feelings was revealed in an
unauthorised recording of a telephone call they made to one
another on 18 December 1989, when they were both still
married to other people, and following the announcement
on 9 December 1992 that the Prince and Princess of Wales
were to separate, both *The Sun* and the *Daily Mirror* began
alluding to the alleged conversation between the Prince of
Wales and Camilla Parker Bowles. They stopped short of
publishing the content, but it was only a matter of time
before it came out. It was a further source of embarrassment
to those involved, including the Queen, who was painfully
aware of the situation. When the Australian magazine *New
Idea* eventually published a graphic transcript, other international outlets, too, began reporting the details. The *Sunday
Mirror* published an extensive transcript. Charles's embarrassment was mixed with relief, as he had known for some
time that the recordings were going to come out; he just
didn't know how or when. It remains one of the most humil-
iating scandals the royal family have had to confront.

Now, just over thirty years later, the incident is still
frequently referred to – not least by Prince Harry, who in
April 2023 included a reference to it in his witness statement
as part of the phone-hacking lawsuit against News Group
Newspapers. He was illustrating why the monarchy may

have sought an agreement between the Palace and the publisher Rupert Murdoch to keep members of the royal family from having to testify about embarrassing stories in court, citing the 'details of an intimate telephone conversation that took place between my father and stepmother in 1989, while he was still married to my mother'. The Duke of Sussex has always regarded Camilla with a great degree of suspicion. Both he and William had begged their father not to marry her, but even so had said they would welcome her into the family.

Harry references Camilla over sixty times in his autobiography *Spare*, and when promoting the tome told *Good Morning America*: 'I see someone who married into this institution and has done everything that she can to improve her own reputation and her own image for her own sake.'

Prior to the phone-call scandal, Andrew Morton's book *Diana: Her True Story*, published the previous June, had been bad enough: Charles had been stunned by the ferocity of the charges levelled against him and was outraged by the part his wife had played in bringing them to print. He saw it as an act of the grossest betrayal. The Queen, desperate to hold her crumbling family together, tried to view matters objectively. She had previously summoned Diana to Buckingham Palace and reminded her of where her duty lay. Diana, tearful and insecure, had wilted under the heavy royal pressure and reluctantly agreed to try. It was to no avail. The Queen has sometimes been slow to act but has always lived by the mantra 'This too shall pass'. In the face of crisis, her response is stillness. 'Storms will come and go, some worse than others,' former prime minister John Major told biographer Robert Hardman. 'But she will always put her head down and plough through them.'

Sir John Major was a good friend to the Queen, and he is one of the only former prime ministers to have been invited to stay at Sandringham, together with his wife, after his term in office. But despite her friendship with both John and Norma, the late Queen never revealed to them her true feelings about the marriage breakdown between Charles and Diana. Her views remained out of bounds to anyone but her close staff and certain members of her family.

With a worldliness that belied her own sheltered upbringing, the Queen was upset not so much by the tapes, nor the adolescent *mots doux* they contained, nor even Morton's book, which was far more damaging to the monarchy as it revealed how uncaring certain members of the family could be. She was most upset by the marital unhappiness that had led up to them.

Charles was less sanguine. Under the tutelage of such gurus as his old friend Sir Laurens van der Post, he had been trying to achieve a spiritual equilibrium. Aware of his faults, such as a tendency for self-pity, petulance, irritability and occasional flares of hot temper, he combated them with huge warmth and compassion. He craved affection and appreciation from both his mother and father, and when he did not receive it he retreated behind a mask of formality, thus becoming unapproachable to them both. The barrage of criticism being aimed in his direction, combined with the unhappiness of his home life with Diana, became an intolerable strain. He felt he was being tangled in knots; this was not the image he wanted for himself or the royal family, not what he wanted for his sons, not what he wanted in a marriage, not what he wanted for Camilla and certainly not what he had ever wanted for Diana.

By his own admission, Charles was not very good at positive thinking. He was, he complained, 'a prisoner' in his own life. And he did what he always did when faced with a situation he could not control – he walked away from it. Camilla was always there for him and didn't depend on him for anything, so when things got too much, he just drove the half hour to Middlewick House in Wiltshire for a few hours with Camilla. It was an escape. He couldn't bear to sit with Diana any more, a member of the Highgrove staff recalls. Diana slammed doors, kicked walls and burst into tears, her frustration and anger so out of control that they were, according to the Highgrove household, 'frightening'. It didn't take long for the Queen to become aware of what was going on through her staff grapevine. She was so concerned by the damage this looming catastrophe would cause the monarchy that she knew she had to overcome her natural reluctance to involve herself directly in disagreeable personal matters. She went down with a bout of flu and took to her bed, which is something she seldom did. Princess Anne, Princess Margaret and Lady Susan Hussey did their best to boost her spirits and remind her that the monarchy had been through worse.

Charles spent much of the autumn of 1992 trying to

explain to his mother (when he could catch her attention) that the damage caused by Diana's accusations – that he was a bad father who took a cruel delight in tormenting her with the blatancy of his affair with Camilla – had made him certain there was little point in continuing with the farce of his marriage. He accused his mother of being out of touch and, in his frustration at trying to make her understand how impossible the marriage had become, he actually lost his temper with her. Charles had arranged a shooting weekend at Sandringham to coincide with William and Harry's exeat from their prep school, Ludgrove, as both boys loved going out on a Sandringham shoot. Quite suddenly and purposefully, Diana refused to bring them and informed Charles she was taking them to Windsor instead. Charles snapped. He telephoned his mother. When she again pleaded patience, he abandoned the training of a lifetime and shouted down the line at the Queen in exasperation: 'Don't you realise? She's mad, mad, mad!' and slammed the receiver down.

The royal family was going up in smoke – quite literally. On 20 November, the Queen's forty-fifth wedding anniversary, Windsor Castle was engulfed by flames. In the private chapel on the first floor of the northeast wing, a faulty spotlight had set fire to a curtain next to the altar. The alarm was raised; at the time, the castle had its own fire department, who arrived on the scene within minutes of being alerted. The fire burned for over twelve hours, causing a massive amount of damage across 115 rooms, including nine state rooms and both St George's Hall and

Brunswick Tower. Five years later, at a cost of £36.5 million, the renovations were finally completed. The monies had been raised by the opening of Buckingham Palace to the public, by private donations and by a private contribution from the Queen of £2 million. The British public, it was discovered, had no interest in contributing to the restoration out of their taxed income.

The most hurtful thing of all for the Queen was that her ability as a mother had been called into question. When three out of four of her children's marriages came to their inevitable end, she asked herself, and her mother and sister, where had she gone wrong? Her self-doubt was compounded by the knowledge that she had also failed to deal with the troubled Diana, whose unhappiness and desperation had culminated in the publication of Andrew Morton's book, which was serialised in the *Sunday Times* from the day before the Garter ceremony and the start of Royal Ascot races – her favourite week of the year.

Worse was to come, as the Queen and Prince Charles now knew. Prime Minister John Major stood up in the House of Commons and said:

'It is announced from Buckingham Palace that, with regret, the Prince and Princess of Wales have decided to separate . . . the decision has been reached amicably and they will continue to participate fully in the upbringing of their children. The Queen and the Duke of Edinburgh, though saddened, understand and sympathise with the difficulties which have led to this decision.'

Just over two years later, in January 1995, Camilla and Andrew Parker Bowles also agreed an amicable divorce. They sold their marital home to Pink Floyd drummer Nick Mason and his wife, and Camilla purchased Ray Mill House, a mere quarter of an hour from Highgrove. Like the previous Prince of Wales, Charles attempted to put his past behind him. He let it be known his work schedule would increase – much to the Queen's relief, as she had complained he was always on holiday. She was concerned for her son but couldn't bring herself to confront him, despite Prince Philip urging her to do so. He felt he could not get involved as Charles believed his father disapproved of anything and everything he did. This was not the case but that was how Charles saw it. He also knew that his parents, and even his adoring grandmother, blamed him for lacking the strength of character to steer Diana out of her traumas. They suspected that by giving up Camilla, he might have saved his marriage – and with it the reputation of the royal family. Instead, the Queen and her husband felt obliged to sit on the fence and watch the marriage implode and along with it all the hard work they had put in over the past forty years.

The Queen also felt that Charles was too grand and spoiled. If he took a shooting party to Sandringham for the weekend, he would have the whole place decorated with huge ferns transported from London in keeping with the Victorian theme of the house. His mother, by contrast, would just have had some potted plants and old-fashioned flower arrangements. Once, when the Queen stayed at

Prince Charles in a Biggles-style flying outfit at RAF Benson in Oxfordshire, where, in July 1979, he fulfilled his ambition to fly a 44-year-old pre-war Tiger Moth biplane. This was one of the Queen's favourite snapshots of her son.

Prince Charles shares a joke with his 101-year-old grandmother
in October 2001 during the unveiling of an Aberdeen Angus bull
sculpture at the Alford Transport Museum in Scotland. The two were
remarkably close and shared an enthusiastic sense of humour.

Diana, Princess of Wales and Queen Elizabeth the Queen Mother
in the carriage procession at Royal Ascot in June 1992. Six months
later, Prime Minister John Major announced the separation of the
Prince and Princess of Wales in the House of Commons.

The Queen and the Prince of Wales appear thoughtful as they watch the races at the Epsom Derby meeting on the fortieth anniversary of the Queen's coronation in 1993.

The Prince of Wales with his eldest son Prince William, enjoying a joke with the waiting media on the Madrisa ski slopes above the Swiss village of Klosters in March 1994.

After a hectic game of polo during Royal Ascot week and the Golden Jubilee celebrations in 2003, the Prince of Wales kisses his delighted mother's hand as she presents him with a prize.

The Queen with the Prince of Wales and the Duchess of Cornwall, all clearly enjoying each other's company in the royal box on the second day of racing at Royal Ascot in June 2013.

Three generations of the royal family: the Queen and the Duke of Edinburgh, their eldest son the Prince of Wales, and his eldest son Prince William at Clarence House before a dinner to mark the fiftieth anniversary of the Queen's coronation in June 2003.

Prince Charles and his extended family pose in the gardens of Clarence House for a delightful official portrait to mark his seventieth birthday in 2018. Seated on the bench next to him is the Duchess of Cornwall with his granddaughter Princess Charlotte, while his grandson Prince George perches on his leg. The Duke and Duchess of Cambridge together with Prince Louis stand behind with the Duke and Duchess of Sussex.

King Charles III salutes alongside his sister Anne, the Princess Royal, during a ceremony at Buckingham Palace to present the new Sovereign's Standard to the Blues and Royals (Royal Horse Guards and 1st Dragoons) on 15 June 2023.

One of the last unofficial photographs of mother and son, taken in October 2021. They are walking to the Balmoral Cricket Pavilion to mark the start of the planting season for the Queen's Green Canopy. Intended to create a network of trees planted in her name to honour seventy years of service, the initiative appealed to both the Queen's and her son's green credentials.

Craigowan on the Balmoral estate during this period, she arrived to find there were no lamps because Charles had taken them all over to Birkhall, the Queen Mother's Scottish residence, where he preferred to stay as it was bigger and more elegant. The Queen was outraged that he had been so selfish and left her without a glimmer of light in the sitting room at Craigowan, with no thought for anyone's comfort except his own. So, she jumped in her Land Rover and drove herself over to Birkhall, retrieved all the lamps that belonged to Craigowan and put them all back where they belonged.

Besides Charles and Diana, the Queen was also worried about her aged mother, who had an abscess on her leg that wouldn't heal. She advised her to spend time in her wheelchair so she could keep the leg up, but the doughty old lady wouldn't listen. Princess Margaret even caught her walking gingerly down a flight of stairs instead of using the lift and admonished her with the words, 'What would your doctor say?' The Queen Mother immediately retorted, 'My doctor is in South Africa, so he won't know!'

Then there were the endless press stories demeaning the monarchy. The Prince of Wales's valet, Ken Stronach, sold his story to the *News of the World*, describing Charles's renowned temper tantrums, how he had sex in the bushes of Highgrove with Camilla and how he had once pulled a washbasin off the wall and smashed it when looking for a cufflink that had fallen down the plughole. It was shocking both due to Stronach's betrayal and to the damage it did to Charles and the reputation of the family. The authorised biography of Charles, written by Jonathan Dimbleby and published in 1994, provided further fodder when Charles revealed to the book's author that he felt his mother had been emotionally distant, that his father was 'beastly' and that both his parents seemed unaware that winning their approval for anything had always eluded him.

That same year the ITV film *Charles: The Private Man, the Public Role* aired and was watched by 14 million viewers. In the film Charles described Camilla as 'a great friend of mine . . . a friend for a very long time' and said that she 'will continue to be a friend for a very long time'. He then admitted he had been faithful to his wife 'until it became irretrievably broken down, us both having tried'.

Prince Charles always believed that he must tell the truth, and that once it was out it would take time to settle but would nonetheless eventually do so. The loser in all this was not the Prince of Wales, but Camilla herself. By November 1995, Diana had added her bit and given the disastrous interview with *Panorama*'s Martin Bashir, who persuaded her she was being lied to and betrayed and put her into a thoroughly paranoid state. Diana's admission on air that her marriage was 'a bit crowded' as there 'were three of us' made sure that Camilla was alone in the face of an extremely hostile world. Her close friend Lady Fiona Lansdowne revealed a little of what Camilla went through during these years when she gave an interview describing the 'incredibly tough' time and stating that it was Camilla's extraordinary strength of character that kept her going:

She was on her own without any protection . . . That was where we could help – she would come and stay with us and the children. I went and got her out of Middlewick one day; there were cameras up against all the windows. But she is resilient: she was brought up with this extraordinary sense of duty where you got on with it, don't whinge, put your best face on and keep going, and it has stood her in very good stead. It was horrible at times, but her sense of humour and know-ledge she had her girlfriends around her got her through.

Camilla needed her girlfriends like never before when the news came through that, in the early hours of 31 August 1997, the Princess of Wales and Dodi Fayed had been in a fatal car accident in a Paris underpass. Dodi had been killed along with the driver, Henri Paul, and Diana was injured. Camilla was among the first people to speak to the Prince after he heard the news. The first reports appeared to suggest that although Dodi had been killed, Diana had only suffered a broken arm. This initial confusion about the facts arose because Diana had been in that nowhere land of being royal but without royal protection. There was no central person to report to except the British Ambassador in Paris, who was awoken from his slumber and telephoned the Queen's deputy private secretary, Robin Janvrin, who was on duty that week.

When it eventually transpired that Diana had died of internal injuries after being transported to the Pitié-Salpêtrière hospital, where surgeons had battled to save her life, things took a very different turn. In shock, Charles called Camilla from Balmoral to tell her, and she spent some time on the phone trying to help him decide what to do. They both knew the public reaction would be to turn against the monarchy and that Charles would get the blame.

At Dodi's father Mohamed Al Fayed's Park Lane head-quarters, the response was far more immediate. Frank Klein, the manager of the Ritz hotel in Paris, had been informed instantaneously of the fatal accident and had contacted London. Shortly afterwards, Al Fayed was informed and his helicopter dispatched to pick him up from his Oxted home. He flew directly to Paris in the early hours of the morning, while his Gulfstream jet was being readied and sent to Le Bourget to remain on standby; being Muslim, Dodi had to be buried before sundown. When Dodi's coffin arrived at the airport to be transported back to Oxted, it was discovered that it wouldn't fit through the door of the jet except by upending it. That was not an option, so in the end it was slid into the helicopter with Al Fayed's brother Ali, while Mohamed flew back to Stansted in the Gulfstream to be ready to receive them. The hearse took Dodi's coffin from Battersea heliport to the nearby Fulham mortuary for the coroner's examination. As Dodi's hearse started to leave the coroner, another hearse passed them inside the gate. It was the body of Diana, Princess of Wales.

The aftermath of Diana's tragic death was a bleak time for Camilla. Once again, she was a prisoner in her own home, and she relied on meals being transported to her from Highgrove by Charles's chef. Charles was doing his best to look after his sons and cancelled all his engagements so he could remain at Highgrove with William and Harry.

Camilla's public entry into Charles's life had been going well. One of their first outings, before Diana's death, had been at the fiftieth birthday party of their mutual friend Lady Sarah Keswick. It was a milestone for Camilla as well as for Charles, because she knew that once they had been seen socialising together, she would become a more credible figure. She realised she was a long way from being accepted as the Prince of Wales's consort, but she had to make the effort for his sake. If it hadn't been for the fickleness of public opinion and the restraining hand of his advisors, Charles would have gone public with Camilla a good deal earlier. He was used to getting his own way and it was Camilla who persuaded him that she was quite happy with how things were. Charles was not satisfied: he wanted them to be photographed together in order to familiarise the public with the situation. For once, the restraining hand of Camilla didn't prevail and it took the authority of the Queen to convince Charles it was not a good idea.

After her divorce, Camilla wasted no time in selling the marital home and buying another property, Ray Mill House. In the meantime she moved into the housekeeper's flat at Bowood House, which was owned by her friends Fiona and Charlie Shelburne. Whenever possible, she would drive to Highgrove to be with Charles, who was desperate to get his divorce from Diana, but at the time – and on the advice of her lawyer – she was holding out for more money. Although Camilla had very little money to live on, having bought her new house, she did at last have a home of her own, which she was going to move into as soon as it was ready. She couldn't afford to do it up but wanted to be able to be independent of Charles and was not keen for another marriage into a world that had rejected her so completely.

Along with everything else, Camilla had family problems to deal with. Her brother-in-law Rick Parker Bowles had said some pretty unpleasant things about her in the press, which upset Camilla as she had always looked after him and tried to help him with his drinking problem, only for him to turn on her. Camilla got on with things the only way she knew how – cheerfully. Before moving house, she decided to go through her wardrobe with her friend Carolyn 'Chubby' Benson, the widow of former racing correspondent and bon viveur Charles Benson. Together they looked at Camilla's dire collection of smart clothes and decided to cut all the frills off Camilla's taffeta evening frocks in an attempt to update them. The pair got the giggles and decided the outfits were all awful, but they were all Camilla had, which made them laugh even more.

The full implication of what it would mean to be Prince Charles's wife frightened Camilla, and she was strident in her refusal to be sucked into the vortex of royal life. She persuaded Charles it would not be a good idea to consider marriage, telling friends the prospect was 'farcical' and that it would never happen as he would always put his duty first. Charles desperately wanted Camilla accepted by his family, especially the Queen, and refused to contemplate her hiding away in her studio – she was a great painter and that is what kept her sane.

It was not an easy transition. In May 2000, relations between the Queen and her son seemed to be at one of their frequent low ebbs. Charles was at Holyroodhouse in his official capacity as Lord High Commissioner – the Queen's personal representative at the General Assembly of the Church of Scotland. Two days into the visit, he invited Camilla to be present by his side at an official dinner. The word from the top was that a Church assembly was not the appropriate place to bring his divorced girlfriend, but something had to be done. The Queen had already made her official disapproval clear by pointedly refusing to attend Charles's fiftieth birthday in 1998; nor was Camilla invited to the Buckingham Palace reception on the eve of his birthday. She was also left off the guest list for any celebrations surrounding the Queen Mother's one hundredth birthday.

A breakthrough came when Camilla was at Charles's side for a lunch party at Highgrove for the exiled King Constantine of Greece. It was his sixtieth birthday and as he was a close friend to the Queen and Prince Philip, it was natural they would be included. They both agreed to attend, along with the King and Queen of Norway, and the King and Queen of Spain, the latter being Constantine's sister, Sofia. Camilla made a low, formal curtsey to the Queen and they enjoyed a brief animated conversation. The Queen knew Camilla would be there and her advisors, in particular Robin Janvrin, had gently suggested it might be an opportunity to dismiss any speculation that they did not get on. For some time, contrary to the then current public opinion, the Queen had thought the couple should get married. Her feeling was it was the only way to end the issue and stop what she called the 'cat and mouse' game the pair were playing. At that time, she didn't think Camilla should 'do' royal duties but did think she should be allowed to be together with Charles to ride and go hunting, visit gardens or whatever they enjoyed doing. She was adamant Camilla should not be Princess of Wales but Duchess of Cornwall, which was exactly what happened. Princess Michael of Kent later reported that the Queen had said the situation had to be resolved, because otherwise what would happen if she were to one day fall off her horse and die? If the Mrs Parker Bowles situation was still unresolved, everything would be a terrible mess.

It eventually took the death of the Queen Mother, on 30 March 2002, to prompt Charles into formalising his relationship with Camilla. The Queen never wanted to do anything to upset 'Mummy' during her long lifetime but now, with her mother's passing, she was free to give the union her blessing. Both the Queen and Philip agreed that Charles should stop procrastinating and get on with it.

Three years later, he did. But as always in his thirty-five-year relationship with Camilla, there were stumbling blocks. The last of these was when Pope John Paul II died, on 2 April 2005, and Charles had to represent the Queen at his funeral in the Vatican on what would have been his wedding day.

Camilla was relieved as she had a serious bout of flu and had been staying at Ray Mill House trying to get herself better in time. The night before the actual wedding, she slept at Clarence House as both Diana and Prince Andrew's then fiancée, Sarah Ferguson, had done before their wedding days. Camilla was still feeling unwell in the morning and it was only the humour of her sister Annabel, who told her that if she didn't get up that she herself would go in her sister's place, that got her out of bed.

The wedding reception was held at Windsor Castle following the service of blessing in St George's Chapel. Camilla's assistant Amanda MacManus recalls that the most emotional moment was when the newlyweds came into the castle after the blessing: 'We all stood waiting to greet them and they both came up the stairs crying. For the first time we said, "Hello, Your Royal Highness." It was a very powerful moment.'

Palace staff provided the 700 guests with delicious tiny sandwiches that could be eaten while standing for the two-hour reception in the state apartments. The Queen had firmly refused to have all the arrangements put in the hands of Charles's controversial ex-valet Michael Fawcett, who was by then his official 'organiser'. She believed it would be inappropriate to have an over-the-top celebration and only agreed to Fawcett doing the flowers inside the chapel, rather than in Windsor Castle itself. Having made herself clear well in advance, the Queen entered into the swing of things, withdrawing only briefly to watch the Grand National on television. She emerged to make a short address to the assembled guests. 'I have two very important announcements to make,' she said. 'I know you all want to know who the winner of the Grand National was. It was Hedgehunter.' She then turned to Charles and Camilla and continued in racing jargon: 'Having cleared Becher's Brook and the Chair, and all kinds of other terrible obstacles, they have come through and I'm very proud and wish them well. My son is home and dry with the woman he loves. They are now on the home straight; the happy couple are now in the winners' enclosure.'

It was a marvellous address and confirmed that the Queen's instincts had been right when she had eventually come to the conclusion that Camilla could well be the making of her son.

'My darling Camilla,' Charles said. 'I can't believe that you married me.' He went on: 'She has stood with me through thick and thin and her optimism and humour have seen me through.'

Camilla needed every ounce of her humour as it became clear that her life was to change much more dramatically than she had anticipated. She soon found she was completely exhausted at the end of each day and would retire to bed early for a bath and to relax with a book, often too tired to even pick up the telephone to her girlfriends, while

Charles carried on working downstairs. Eventually Camilla found the demands placed on her quite stimulating, as she explained: 'Sometimes you get up in the morning and think you can't do it, and you just have to. The minute you stop it's like a balloon, you run out of puff – you sort of collapse in a heap. I think you live on adrenaline.' Camilla revealed that the key to keeping up with her full diary is to stay positive and to 'just get on with it', which she says is a 'very British thing'.

The Queen recognised this in Camilla. She saw how her workload increased and noticed how the many charities she supported genuinely meant something to her in a way that her late husband's had meant so much to him. In the documentary *Prince Philip: The Royal Family Remembers*, shown after his death, Camilla gave a rare interview explaining that she had used Philip as a model for her own role as a future consort. 'I've learned by watching him,' she admitted. 'I saw the way he supported the Queen. Not in a flashy sort of way, but just by doing it quietly, following along behind.' Camilla got along well with Philip, especially after his retirement, when he had more time. They would talk about books together; he had passed patronage of the BookTrust on to her when he retired. Camilla was an excellent listener and genuinely enjoyed hearing about his life and the diverse people he had met and how amusing he was when describing them. Like Camilla, the Duke was a straight talker and the Queen appreciated how patient her daughter-in-law had been with her irascible husband.

Today, staff working at Clarence House say what a happy

atmosphere there is. The house is full of laughter and, before the Queen died, Charles and Camilla used to give a party for all the staff who had helped them over the year so they could watch Trooping the Colour. The invitation was sent out from the Duchess and a special viewing area was reserved outside the garden walls on the Mall. When the ceremony was over, the guests could go onto the roof of Clarence House to watch the flypast before being treated to drinks and canapés in the garden. It was a wonderful invitation, which was originally instigated by the late Queen Elizabeth the Queen Mother, and it is one of the many traditions Charles and Camilla continued to honour.

Camilla is now at the heart of royal life, whether it is something she wanted or not. Her father, the late Major Bruce Shand, used to tease her by calling her 'la Reine'. But it was never something she coveted or wanted. Everything she does is out of love for her husband and the desire she has always had to support him.

When he gave his first address as King, from the Blue Drawing Room of Buckingham Palace, Charles complained that the room was too hot, and the windows had to be opened. The director was loathe to do so due to a helicopter circling above, but he had no choice and the windows were opened. Immediately, the noise from the helicopter stopped, and the King commenced his address.

It was word perfect and captured the dramatic mood of the moment. One of the two cameramen later recalled that immediately afterwards Camilla, who was standing out of view, moved to Charles's side, hugged him and told him how wonderful he had been. 'That,' the cameraman recounted to me, 'is her secret. She has huge admiration for him and is full of genuine praise. What man can resist that?'

There is little doubt that Queen Camilla will continue to be the strength behind the crown, just as Elizabeth Bowes-Lyon was the strength behind her husband when he became King George VI. They are quite different situations, but the end result was that both women made their husbands happy and contented, and the task of kingship less onerous. It was not just the two women's people skills – the easy, open and friendly manner they both shared – but their desire to never overshadow their husbands. It may be an old-fashioned view, but it is one that works.

11

OUR COMMONWEALTH

Prince Philip called it her 'family'. Nelson Mandela called it 'a rainbow organisation'. But both credited the late Queen as the one person who had kept the Commonwealth together. From the moment it came into being, in 1949, and the terms 'British Empire' and 'Imperial' gradually began to disappear in favour of the 'Commonwealth of Nations', the members of the Commonwealth have been linked by their voluntary acceptance of the crown as head of the organisation.

King George VI had talked with great enthusiasm about it with his eldest daughter, Princess Elizabeth, and she understood that part of her inheritance would be to ensure that his vision of the new Commonwealth came to fruition. His concept of how it would work, matched with her determination to make it happen, became the dominant aspect of her queenship. Her father, the last Emperor of India and a man she loved and respected, had by his vision ensured the Commonwealth was always to be a priority for her.

'If we all go forward together with an unwavering faith, a high courage, and a quiet heart, we shall be able to make of this ancient Commonwealth, which we all love so dearly, an even grander thing – more free, more prosperous, more happy and a more powerful influence for good in the world,' Princess Elizabeth had said in a speech broadcast from Cape Town on her twenty-first birthday. When she became Queen five years later, she would spend the remainder of her long reign doing exactly that.

At the end of the Second World War, in which so many men and women of the British Empire volunteered to leave their homelands and fight for the Allies in Europe and elsewhere, the movement of British colonies towards independence was growing. The modern Commonwealth was born on 27 April 1949, when the leaders of its member nations issued a document, the London Declaration, in which the phrase 'common allegiance to the Crown' was dropped as a prerequisite for Commonwealth membership.

The young new Queen had a magic touch. She was less formal than her father when she was travelling in the realms of the Commonwealth and many of the trappings of majesty were put aside when she met people of all types and nationalities. It wasn't only the people that appreciated her; the late Nelson Mandela noted that 'very-difficult-to-please heads of state really appreciate her as Head of the Commonwealth'.

She was popular and non-controversial, young, beautiful

215

and enthusiastic, and her appearances hailed a new beginning – what exactly for, no one could say, but after the
years of war, her youth represented a positive future.

When she made her first visit to Australia in 1954 with
the Duke of Edinburgh, her 'handsome and cheerful'
husband, by her side, tens of thousands lined the streets
in crowds of twenty deep to catch a glimpse of her as she
drove by. In the cities, onlookers fainted in the rush, while
out in the bush families waited for hours in the heat on
roads usually empty to see her pass by.

There were times when it was more than the Queen was
able to handle. She came from a background as sheltered
as they come, and she was painfully shy. She was still only
twenty-seven, in a distant land, and her children were half
a world away. After one particularly gruelling day, her
composure nearly deserted her. She had been gaped at,
waved at, cheered at, blinded by old-fashioned camera
bulbs and had her hand shaken until it was bruised and
aching. She was tired and overwrought, and her crowded
schedule had allowed her no privacy. In a snatched moment
alone with Philip and on the verge of tears, she turned and
in a trembling voice demanded to know: 'Why is everyone
so boring, boring, boring?'

Prince Philip came to the rescue. He had remained in
the background throughout their trip, amusing himself
by waving to drunks hanging on to lamp-posts outside
pubs as they drove by, who then collapsed to the ground
when they let go to wave back. His description of this
entertainment immediately made the Queen laugh. That,

he considered in those early days, was what he was there for.

As the world changed, so did feelings about the Queen, and some Australians came to regard her as aloof and cold, while the Duke of Edinburgh was thought of as 'cranky, conservative and difficult', in historian Stuart Macintyre's words. A leading politician of the time has even described Philip as 'a monumental pain in the arse'. In the early days of the Commonwealth, no one would ever have thought to brazenly express such views. Everything was very correct, with enormous protocol.

Neville Wran, former Labour premier of New South Wales in Australia, remembers the first time he met the Queen in the late 1970s, when Scottish devolution was on the agenda. He was trying to think of something to say to her and show her how up-to-date he was and made the mistake of asking for her views on the subject. 'A block of ice descended from the ceiling,' he recalled. 'If she didn't like the question, she had a terrific technique of just not answering.' On another occasion, Wran was sitting across from the Queen at Buckingham Palace and engaged in conversation with her, while Prince Philip was talking to someone else. And then Philip butted into their conversation with an inane comment. 'The Queen was marvellous in the way she handled him. She said in so many words: "You don't know what you're talking about. Let us just get on with it." She did it very politely.'

In the early days, the Queen's first Commonwealth Secretary-General, Arnold Smith, wrote of her quiet acceptance of any 'reverses' – he would often have to tell her that another colony was about to seek independence and she always accepted the inevitable with calmness. He contrasted her attitude with that of her grandfather George V, who exploded with rage when he discovered that Canada had signed a fishing treaty with the USA without first consulting him. George VI was not quite so stoical as the Queen when the British Raj came to an end in India. Throughout his reign from 1936 he signed his name 'George RI' for Rex Imperator or 'King Emperor'. He had to drop the 'I' under the terms of the 1947 Indian Independence Act. At the same time, the inscription 'Ind. Imp.' for 'Indiae Imperator' (Emperor of India) disappeared from British coins of the realm. When Queen Mary first received a letter from her son without the GRI signature, she wrote a comment on it: 'The first time Bertie wrote me a letter with the I for Emperor of India left out, very sad.'

Today any country can apply for membership of the Commonwealth; the last two countries to join were Gabon and Togo, in 2022. Fundamentals that have come down from the old British Empire include a civil service, the rule of law, democracy and the English language. Papua New Guinea, which joined in 1975, does not quite fit into this last category as its official language is 'pidgin English', or 'Tok Pisin'. Charles, who is now their King, has visited the islands several times, including for the Queen's Diamond Jubilee, when he had the charming official title of 'Number One Picaninny Belong Missus Queen'.

Prince Charles was already popular in the Commonwealth, especially in Australia as he had been to Geelong Grammar School's Timbertop campus in Victoria. From his first visit he remained fond of Australia and Australians, so much so that there was a period when thought was seriously given to him becoming Governor-General of Australia. Malcolm Fraser was prime minister at the time and thought, 'Why not?' But it was never to be, as the idea of having a non-Australian Governor-General was deemed unworkable.

The Queen established an annual message to the Commonwealth on Commonwealth Day, which falls on the second Monday of March and is marked by peoples all over the world. In London it is celebrated with a service at Westminster Abbey attended by the monarch and the rest of the royal family. In his own first Commonwealth Day message as monarch, King Charles spoke from the great pulpit at Westminster Abbey instead of relying on a pre-recorded message. Charles recalled his mother's 'particular pride' in Commonwealth Day and said: 'The Commonwealth has been a constant in my own life, and yet its diversity continues to amaze and inspire me. Its near boundless potential as a force for good in the world demands our highest ambition; its sheer scale challenges us to unite and be bold.'

Delivering the address in person from the Abbey was a dramatic statement of Charles's intention to continue his mother's important role within the Commonwealth. He had already delivered a message from his mother, when she was too frail to attend the 2022 Commonwealth Games. The Queen believed in the personal touch, but in the last months of her long life she found moving around almost impossible.

In the past, the Queen always invited the leaders of each member state to a large meeting, usually a lunch or dinner, held every other year, known as the Commonwealth Heads of Government Meeting (CHOGM). In doing so she has had to spend time with some very unsavoury characters. When Major General Idi Amin took control of Uganda in a military coup in 1971, the British Foreign Office was keen to forge a relationship with him in spite of his human rights abuses. The Queen entertained Amin to lunch at Buckingham Palace, during which she became aware of his intention to invade Tanzania, a neighbouring Commonwealth nation. The Foreign Office was immediately informed and relations with Amin broke down; he did not appear at the next three CHOGMs. During this period, he was estimated to have massacred some 300,000 people. One of his favourite ways of getting rid of any political enemies was to take them up in the presidential helicopter and push them out from a great height.

Robert Mugabe of Zimbabwe was another leader who was initially welcomed with an official state visit. Mugabe drove his country into dire poverty while he enriched himself and his cronies. He later withdrew Zimbabwe from the Commonwealth when he discovered it was about to be thrown out. In 1973, the British government invited Mobutu Sese Seko, the corrupt president of Zaire, to a state visit. According to royal biographer Robert Hardman, 'an extensive briefing document had been sent to the Queen explaining how he hanged his rivals and extorted the wealth of the nation'. As Head of State, the Queen had to put up with him and his excessive demands as there was hope for Britain to secure a £34 million contract from him. What the Queen would not and could not do was put up with his wife smuggling her pet dog into the palace, which was discovered when she ordered some raw meat from the kitchens. The Queen was 'enraged', recalled her former private secretary Sir William Heseltine, and the dog was taken to quarantine kennels, with the Queen's corgis taken to Windsor. To make matters worse, Mobutu tried to excuse the dog incident by saying it was British by birth and had been brought to London so it could see its native town. Members of the royal household had never seen the Queen so angry or upset and it was the talk of the Palace for months afterwards.

King Charles III is now Head of the Commonwealth. It remains to be seen which, if any, of the fifteen realms of which he is King will now choose to abandon the crown and move to a republican system.

In a statement issued by Buckingham Palace in November 1999, the Queen was at pains to emphasise that she thought Australia's membership was something the Australians should determine and that she wouldn't be offended if they chose another route. 'I have always made it clear that the future of the monarchy in Australia is an issue for the Australian people and them alone to decide, by democratic and constitutional means. My family and I would, of course, have retained our deep affection for Australia and Australians everywhere, whatever the outcome.'

As King, Charles will never have his mother's experience of the Commonwealth. He couldn't possibly do so as he knew it was her 'baby' and, as much as he may have wanted to, he knew it was a bad idea to interfere or indeed even proffer one of his opinions. 'He did not trample on the Queen's Commonwealth turf,' Sir Shridath 'Sonny' Ramphal, former Secretary-General explained, 'so he never became a royal insider in Commonwealth affairs. He has not been an intimate part of it because he felt very consciously that the Queen regarded the Commonwealth as her thing.'

As he got older, Charles's interests were very much more focused on India and the Middle East, where he was feted like the king he would become. He disliked long-haul flights, as did the Duchess of Cornwall, and the thought of visiting some of the further-flung outposts of the Commonwealth did not appeal to him, so his office made every possible excuse not to travel so far.

Charles opened his first Commonwealth conference in November 2013, in Sri Lanka. It was considered too far for the 87-year-old Queen and 92-year-old Duke of Edinburgh to travel, so Charles, who had not yet been appointed the

Queen's Commonwealth successor, was responsible for giving a good impression. His former valet Michael Fawcett supervised the decoration of the extravagant welcoming banquet, which spared no expense. The Duchess of Cornwall was resplendent in the Queen Mother's tiara and turned her legendary charm onto as many of the Commonwealth leaders as she could. Despite this significant charm offensive, the conference was not considered a total success and it was suspected that Charles had not truly got the sense of the requirements of the Commonwealth leaders.

Two years later, in 2015, the Prince of Wales and Duchess of Cornwall accompanied the Queen and the Duke of Edinburgh to the island of Malta in a further subtle bid to encourage the Commonwealth leaders to accept the Prince of Wales as the Queen's successor. In her opening speech the Queen reminded her audience:

> Prince Philip and I first came to live here in 1949, the same year in which the Commonwealth was founded. The sixty-six years since then have seen a vast expansion of human freedom: the forging of independent nations and new Commonwealth members, many millions of people sprung from the trap of poverty, and the unleashing of the talents of a global population. I have been privileged to witness this transformation, and to consider its purpose.

At the very end of her speech, she mentioned her son alongside her husband when she said:

223

Prince Philip has brought boundless energy and commitment, for which I am indebted. Nor could I wish to have been better supported and represented in the Commonwealth than by the Prince of Wales, who continues to give so much to it with great distinction.

It was not until 2018, when the Commonwealth Heads of Government Meeting was held in London, that the Queen invited the leaders to a 'retreat' hosted by herself at Windsor Castle. It had been announced at the London meeting that it was her 'sincere wish' to be succeeded by her son, and when the Commonwealth leaders returned from the castle, a statement from the leaders confirming this news was issued:

We recognise the role of the Queen in championing the Commonwealth and its people. The next head of the Commonwealth shall be his Royal Highness Prince Charles, the Prince of Wales.

It was left to the then prime minister, Theresa May, to declare that the decision had been unanimous:

His Royal Highness has been a proud supporter of the Commonwealth for more than four decades and has spoken passionately about the organisation's unique diversity. And it is fitting that, one day, he will continue the work of his mother, Her Majesty the Queen.

At the end of the 2018 summit, after Prince Charles had worked hard to underline his knowledge of the organisation to its various and varied leaders, he explained that the Commonwealth had been 'a fundamental feature of my life for as long as I can remember, beginning with my first visit to Malta when I was just five years old'.

The Commonwealth has grown up alongside King Charles and he can relate to it without having to take on the nurturing role that was required of the Queen in 1949. When Charles went on the Queen's behalf to the CHOGM in Rwanda in June 2022, he chose to speak about the suffering caused by the historic slave trade. 'To unlock the power of our common future, we must also acknowledge the wrongs which have shaped our past,' he said. 'I cannot describe the depths of my personal sorrow at the suffering of so many, as I continue to deepen my own understanding of slavery's enduring impact.'

Maybe he was right, maybe he was wrong, but he saw it as his duty that 'Imperialist delusions' about the modern Commonwealth were dispelled.

The outcome of the cultural battles of the next few years is now in Charles's hands. It is an unenviable challenge but one he will face with fortitude, as he has the many other problems surrounding the survival of our planet and life as we know it. Part of the respect that the Commonwealth had for the Queen was the fact that she had been there for so long and knew what she was talking about. It cannot apply in the same way to the King, but he will make up for it in other ways.

When she came to the throne, the young Queen wanted to ensure that the memory of her father's founding of the Commonwealth would be upheld. She did so with great dignity and commanded universal respect. As for Charles, Sonny Ramphal has said: 'It is going to be a very different kind of role, but I believe he will rise to the challenge.' The King will surely do everything he can to keep the Commonwealth going in memory of his mother, as it was her fervent wish he should do so.

During the first Commonwealth tour of his reign, in Kenya at the end of October 2023, the King did just that. His speech at the state banquet highlighted the 'special meaning' Kenya has had for his family, especially his late mother, not least because it is where she found out she was Queen. According to the *Sunday Times*, Charles also 'banged the drum for UK plc with a key African trading partner, championed the environment and when discussing the shadow cast by colonial rule, carefully trod a diplomatic tightrope'.

The King stressed the importance of holding the Commonwealth together regardless of which realms choose to keep him as head of state and which declare independence. 'It is, above all, a family of nations,' he said, 'and the important thing, I think, is to retain if we can and maintain that family feel.'

12

OUR FAITH

The late Queen's deep Christian faith was a constant throughout her life. She never saw going to church as a duty, it was something she enjoyed and always had done. She loved traditional hymns and preferred the all-embracing words of the Authorised Version of the Bible, which appealed to her pragmatic and conservative values.

The King's faith, although equally deep, has been arrived at by a more circuitous route. Prince Charles has committed much time to studying the other great religions of the world, endlessly questioning and probing into their different philosophies.

'I am one of those people who searches,' Charles once said about his spiritual quest. 'I am interested in pursuing a path if I can find it through the thickets.'

His sons, the Prince of Wales and the Duke of Sussex, have few of the powerful religious ties that were so relevant in the life of their grandmother and infiltrated into the spirituality of their father. Harry revealed in his autobiography that he is not religious despite his 'pa' being someone who 'prayed every night'. At William and Catherine's wedding, they vowed they would never forget the importance of faith in the turmoil of their everyday life.

The Queen's relationship with the Church of England was symbolised at her coronation in 1953, when she was anointed by the then Archbishop of Canterbury, Geoffrey Fisher, who asked her to maintain the laws of God. 'The coronation was a deeply moving, spiritual experience for her,' the Queen's cousin, the late Margaret Rhodes, recalled. 'She looked like a nun being married to the church,' Anne Glenconner, the Queen's former maid-of-honour, commented. 'It was a very, very moving moment,' she recalled.

The Rt Revd Michael Mann, a former Dean of Windsor, also recalled that the Queen was 'a person of very deep faith':

She looked on the coronation in the way in which the coronation is intended. It is a statement. She believed that when she was crowned, she was set aside, consecrated for a particular purpose. When I retired, I had to go and see her and say I was going to retire and the only comment I got was: 'It's all right for you. I can't.' And this feeling of being set aside to a particular task for the whole of her life was something that the coronation set upon her like a seal.

After her anointing by the Archbishop of Canterbury, the Queen proceeded to the High Altar and made her solemn oath to God. Laying her right hand upon the Bible, she kneeled and declared: 'The things which I have here before promised, I will perform and keep. So help me, God.' Then she kissed the Bible and signed the oath.

At his coronation in 2023, the oath sworn by King Charles differed in one respect from that sworn by his mother – namely the territories they reigned over. While the Queen had cited a long list of countries and regions where she would also be monarch, King Charles promised 'to govern the peoples of the United Kingdom of Great Britain and Northern Ireland, your other realms and territories'. In the seventy years since Queen Elizabeth's coronation, many countries have removed the British monarch as Head of State.

As a young princess, the future monarch was brought up to say her prayers both in the morning before breakfast and in the evening before going to bed. Church on Sunday was part of her routine throughout her long life, wherever she happened to be. At Windsor she attended services at St George's Chapel, founded in 1348 by King Edward III. Much more intimate is the late Queen's private chapel within the castle itself. Destroyed by fire in 1992, it was rebuilt with only twenty-five seats. The new organ had to be designed to fit into a very small triangular loft. She also liked to go to the private Chapel of All Saints by Royal Lodge. When her mother was still alive, they would always convene for a sherry at Royal Lodge after the Sunday service, and when Princess Beatrice married Edoardo Mapelli Mozzi in July 2020, the limited small service was at the Chapel of All Saints. It was also the venue for the joint christening of the Queen's youngest great-grandchildren, August Brooksbank and Lucas Tindall, the sons of her grandchildren Eugenie and Zara.

Watching the extended royal family attend church on Christmas Day is an important part of the Christmas ritual to many, especially to locals in Norfolk. Crowds turn out in all kinds of weather to greet the royal family as they attend St Mary Magdalene Church, 400 yards from the big house on the Sandringham estate. King Charles has diligently followed the tradition of taking the family to this church on Christmas Day and throughout the holiday period. The church has been the site of many royal christenings, including those of King George VI, Lady Diana Spencer, Princess Eugenie of York and most recently Princess Charlotte of Wales.

When at Balmoral, the royal family have the family pew at Crathie Kirk, a small Church of Scotland parish church. The Princess Royal married her second husband, Timothy Laurence, at the church because she was divorced and, at the time, not permitted to marry in the Church of England. The Queen recalled what a happy occasion it was and a bright light in the gloomy year she called her 'annus horribilis'.

To the Queen, her faith was all-important. 'It was not just a question of duty for her, it was very much part of the fabric of her life,' a former chaplain at Windsor remarked. 'She loved Matins, and the words of the Prayer Book had real meaning for her.'

Time and again in her Christmas Day broadcasts, the Queen stressed the importance of her religious beliefs and her faith in Jesus Christ. However, in the 1960s she began to play down the specifically Christian aspects of the celebration. It was all part of her early acknowledgement of the importance of all faiths, which in later years she came back to again and again.

'Many will have been inspired by Jesus's simple but powerful teaching,' she reminded us in the Millennium year. 'Love God and love thy neighbour as thyself – in other words, treat others as you would like them to treat you. His great emphasis was to give spirituality a practical purpose. For me the teachings of Christ and my own personal accountability before God provide a framework in which I try to lead my life.' Two years later she was saying the same thing in a different way: 'I know just how much I rely on my own faith to guide me through the good times and the bad. Each day is a new beginning, I know that the only way to live my life is to try to do what is right, to take the long view, to give of my best in all that the day brings, and to put my trust in God.'

Accordingly, reconciliation became a recurring theme in her broadcasts. There is little doubt that if the Queen had been younger and stronger, she would have fought to find a way to help the Duke and Duchess of Sussex from being at loggerheads with the rest of the family. 'Reconciliation is a Christian virtue but one that we can all relate to,' she noted back in 2014 as she summarised her faith: 'For me, the life of Jesus Christ, the Prince of Peace, whose birth we celebrate today, is an inspiration and an anchor in my life. A role model of reconciliation and forgiveness, he stretched out his hands in love, acceptance, and healing. Christ's example has taught me to seek to respect and value all people, of whatever faith or none.'

After the death of the Queen, in September 2022, a number of distinguished religious leaders spoke about her strong beliefs. The leader of the Catholic Church in Ireland, Archbishop Eamon Martin, said that it had always been very clear to him that Queen Elizabeth II was a woman of deep personal faith. 'She was unafraid to be a strong, personal and courageous witness to the teachings of Christ,' he said. 'Here was a woman who lived her faith – who served the Lord at every moment of her life and who really wrote faith into everything that she thought, said and did.' He said that he was extremely grateful for the efforts she made in crossing 'safe boundaries' and interacting with the Catholic Church, noting that she had met five different Popes during her reign. He added: 'That, to me, shows that she wanted to show that she was not in any way narrow in her understanding of her Christianity, she was prepared to accept and support all of those within the Christian faith, and outside.'

The Chief Rabbi, Ephraim Mirvis, said it was clear through all his meetings with the Queen, including the time he accompanied her to the Nazi concentration camp at Bergen-Belsen in Germany, that her interest in his faith went far beyond duty. 'I could see the extent of her connection with Jews and Judaism and her concern for the safety of Jews,' he said.

In a telegram to King Charles III on the death of his mother, Pope Francis wrote: 'I willingly join all who mourn her loss in praying for the late Queen's eternal rest, and in paying tribute to her life of unstinting service to the good of the Nation and the Commonwealth, her example of devotion to duty, her steadfast witness of faith in Jesus Christ and her firm hope in his promises.'

The Muslim leader Imam Qari Muhammad Asim, chairman of the Mosques and Imams National Advisory Board, said: 'In increasingly uncertain times, the reassuring presence of the Queen has been a source of continuity, strength and stability for our country and beyond. British Muslims value HM the Queen's respect for other people's beliefs and concern for welfare of others throughout her long reign.'

Lord Singh of Wimbledon, Director of the Network of Sikh Organisations in the UK, agreed when he said:

Her life was one of selfless service to her subjects, an unparalleled service conducted with both dignity and humility throughout her seventy-year reign . . . I recall the privilege of accompanying Her Majesty during her first visit to a gurdwara, in Leicester in 2002. It was during her Golden Jubilee celebrations that she made clear that she was the sovereign for all her people, and that our different religions show that God's love extends in equal measure to the whole of humanity; a resonant echo of Sikh teachings that shows the important commonalities between our different faiths. Her Majesty's commitment to the service of others, contribution to society and humility in all she did, are qualities that Sikhs aspire to embody in their lives. Sikhs will always remember her with love and affection.

Billy Graham, the world-famous American evangelist, who died in 2018, met the Queen many times and they established an unlikely friendship. On one occasion, when he and his wife were staying at Balmoral, the Queen was putting together material for her Christmas address, to be broadcast on Christmas Day 1975. The Queen asked Graham to come and listen to her practise her speech by a pond in the grounds, where she tossed a stone into the water. The Queen explained that, if you throw a stone into a pool, the ripples go on spreading outwards. 'A big stone can cause waves, but even the smallest pebble changes the whole pattern of the water. Our daily actions are like those ripples – each one makes a difference, even the smallest . . . The combined effect can be enormous. If enough grains of sand are dropped into one side of a pair of scales they will, in the end, tip it against a lump of lead.'

Graham loved the Queen's wisdom, much of which was gained from her extensive knowledge of the Bible. 'I always found her very interested in the Bible and its message,' Graham said. 'After preaching at Windsor one Sunday, I was sitting next to the Queen at lunch. I told her I had been undecided until the last minute about my choice of sermon and had almost preached on the healing of the crippled man in John 5. Her eyes sparkled and she bubbled over with enthusiasm, as she could do on occasion. "I wish you had!" she exclaimed. "That is my favourite story".'

Prince Charles's religious life began when he was christened only a month after his birth, on 15 December 1948, by Geoffrey Fisher, then the Archbishop of Canterbury. The ceremony took place in the Music Room at Buckingham Palace, and his mother, then Princess Elizabeth, chose the first hymn to reflect the sacred significance of the event: 'Holy, Holy, Holy!'. It was a grand affair, and among his godparents were two kings, one queen, a princess and a prince.

From the time Charles went to school at Gordonstoun, where he heard Mervyn Stockwood, the Bishop of Southwark, preach a sermon, he has always been spiritually curious. He began corresponding with Stockwood, who introduced him to parapsychology, the study of the supernatural. He continued his correspondence with Stockwood while an undergraduate at Cambridge. Stockwood believed that the miracles of Jesus demonstrated 'the Saviour's oneness with nature', one of the starting points of Charles's lifelong interest in the natural world. Mervyn Stockwood was certainly the most colourful and controversial diocesan bishop of his generation and, given his contradictory character, probably one of the most popular and successful. He certainly had the attention of the teenage Prince of Wales.

At Cambridge Charles was influenced by another English cleric, Harry Williams, Dean of Chapel at Trinity College, who introduced him to the works of Carl Jung. For Jung, the purpose of life was individuation, which involves pursuing one's own vision of the truth, and, in so doing, realising one's fullest potential as a human being.

In his mid-twenties, Charles fell under the influence of Laurens van der Post, the South African-born writer, explorer and self-proclaimed clairvoyant. Van der Post was a Jungian mystic who went on to become spiritual advisor to Prince Charles for more than twenty years; it is reputed that he taught Charles to talk to his plants. When Prince William was christened, in 1982, Charles made van der Post one of his godfathers.

Charles was greatly influenced by van der Post's book *The Lost World of the Kalahari*, in which primitive man's spiritual connection with nature is explored. He planned a seven-week trip to the Kalahari Desert with van der Post to spend time with the tribesmen, but the Foreign Office advised him not to go on the grounds of security. Instead, he travelled with van der Post to spend a week in the Aberdare mountains in Kenya, where they lived close to nature and spent their time deep in conversation. Van der Post's wife, Ingaret, also encouraged Charles to write down his dreams, which she would then interpret in Jungian fashion. The friendship with the van der Posts left a lasting impression on Charles's faith. The Rt Revd James Jones, who during his fifteen-year tenure as Bishop of Liverpool regularly prayed with Prince Charles, recalled: 'I once heard him tell someone that he spoke up for respecting the natural world for the glory of God.'

Van der Post was the first in a series of mystics with

whom Prince Charles became involved. Islamic teaching and art, reincarnation, Plato's philosophy and Sufism were all subjects brought to Charles's attention by different gurus at different times. At one time he interested himself in Buddhism and for a while became a vegetarian and gave up shooting, a phase that did not last long. But he did give his matching pair of Purdey shotguns to his brother, Prince Andrew.

For more than two decades Prince Charles was patron of the Oxford Centre for Islamic Studies, where in 1993 he gave a speech on Islam and the West that was reprinted in newspapers across the Middle East. Farhan Nizami, the centre's director, said at the time, 'I don't think there is another major figure in the Western world who has as high a standing as he has in the Muslim world. I would describe him as a friend of Muslims.'

The Most Revd Vincent Nichols, the Archbishop of Westminster, said that Prince Charles seemed 'thoroughly at home' on his visits to Westminster Cathedral, the seat of British Catholicism. 'I don't sense any discomfort when he is in a Catholic Church,' he says. 'I am told occasionally when he is abroad, he happily goes to Mass, and is at peace with that.' In his desire to bridge the gap between what he called 'the destructive gulf' of Catholics and Protestants, Charles took a step too far while on an official visit to Italy in 1985, however. He made arrangements to attend Pope John Paul's domestic Eucharist at the Vatican but failed to notify the Queen's private secretary, Sir Philip Moore, with whom he did not get on and who he described as 'an oily creep'. The Queen heard about the plans at the last minute and called Charles to Buckingham Palace. He was forced to cancel his plans to attend a Catholic Mass in the Vatican at the last minute as it was not considered to be appropriate for the future head of the Church of England.

In 1968, Charles made the first of many pilgrimages to the Orthodox monasteries on Mount Athos in northern Greece. The community comprises twenty monasteries and the settlements that they depend on, housing about 2,000 Eastern Orthodox monks from Greece and many other countries who live an ascetic life isolated from the rest of the world. The monasteries feature a rich collection of well-preserved artefacts, rare books, ancient documents and artworks of immense historical value. Charles's father, Prince Philip, was baptised at the monasteries of Mount Athos and his grandmother, Princess Alice of Greece, became an Orthodox nun. Charles was influenced to visit Mount Athos by his painting instructor, Derek Hill, who used to make an annual pilgrimage to the monasteries. Although Charles was accompanied by his protection officer and would arrive with a satellite telephone and a considerable amount of luggage, he was expected to follow the daily routine of the monks. Charles spent much of his time there in contemplation and silent prayer. In his spiritual retreats in the monasteries, he said he was inspired by the perennial wisdom of the Athonite fathers and that he could 'retrieve his lost balance' when visiting there.

In the gardens of his country house, Highgrove in Gloucestershire, the King has created an area specifically for contemplation and private prayer. The Stumpery, as it is called, consists of an area of tree stumps, ferns, wood sculptures and two rustic Greek-style temples inspired by Victorian gardening techniques. When Prince Philip first saw this unusual area, he asked his son, 'When are you going to set fire to this lot?', perfectly demonstrating the gulf of misunderstanding between them. Charles has also created a private temple of worship at Highgrove, called the Sanctuary, which was built in 1999. The architect, Charles Morris, devised a system of four door handles that will only open the door to the Sanctuary if turned in a special way known only to Charles and a few of his closest friends. Above the door of the Sanctuary is the inscription 'Lighten our darkness, we beseech thee, O Lord'.

Shortly after his accession to the crown, King Charles held a reception in the Bow Room at Buckingham Palace for more than thirty faith leaders from various religions. Speaking to his guests, Charles, who is now Supreme Governor of the Church of England, confirmed a 'determination to carry out my responsibilities as sovereign of all communities around this country and the Commonwealth and in a way which reflects the world in which we now live.' He continued:

As a member of the Church of England, my Christian beliefs have love at their very heart. By my most profound convictions, therefore – as well as by my position as Sovereign – I hold myself bound to respect those who follow other spiritual paths, as well as those who seek to live their lives in accordance with secular ideals. The beliefs that flourish in, and contribute to, our richly diverse society differ. They, and our society, can only thrive through a clear collective commitment to those vital principles of freedom of conscience, generosity of spirit and care for others, which are, to me, the essence of our nationhood. I am determined, as King, to preserve and promote those principles across all communities, and for all beliefs, with all my heart.

He added:

It is my duty to protect the diversity of our country, including by protecting the space for faith itself and its practice through the religions, cultures, traditions and beliefs to which our hearts and minds direct us as individuals. This diversity is not just enshrined in the laws of our country, it is enjoined by my own faith. This was the foundation of everything my beloved mother did for our country, over her years as our Queen. It has been the foundation of my own work as Prince of Wales. It will continue to be the foundation of all my work as King.

It isn't only King Charles who has sought to make the Church of England more inclusive towards other religions. At a Lambeth Palace ecumenical meeting hosted by the Archbishop of Canterbury in February 2012, the Queen, speaking as Supreme Governor of the Church of England in her Diamond Jubilee year, said: 'The concept of our established Church is occasionally misunderstood and, I believe, commonly under-appreciated. Its role is not to defend Anglicanism to the exclusion of other religions. Instead, the Church has a duty to protect the free practice of all faiths in this country.'

In November 2015, following a service of Holy Communion in Westminster Abbey, the Archbishop of Canterbury, Justin Welby, welcomed the Queen and the Duke of Edinburgh to the Inaugural Group of Sessions of the Tenth General Synod. In her formal address to the Synod, the Queen again spoke of reconciliation when she said:

St Paul reminds us that all Christians, as ambassadors for Christ, are entrusted with the ministry of reconciliation. Spreading God's word and the onerous but rewarding task of peace-making and conflict resolution are important parts of that ministry. So, too, is the Church of England's particular vocation to work in partnership with those of other faiths and none, to serve the common good in this land.

The first-ever Black Archbishop of York, Ugandan-born John Sentamu, summed it up very beautifully when he described a private moment with the Queen back in 2018. Sentamu said the Queen comforted him by praying during their meeting, in which he asked permission to step down as Archbishop of York. 'I went with a huge burden, and I knelt down and I said, "Your Majesty, please pray for me."

So, I put my hands together and she put hers together outside mine and closed her eyes. She was completely silent for three minutes. And at the end she just said, "Amen." When I got up, the burden had lifted.'

The moment King Charles acceded the throne on 8 September 2022, he appeared transformed. He was obviously moved by his mother's death, but he also appeared to be filled with a vital new strength she had somehow passed to him. He was emotional, but he was completely in control when he made his first powerful address to the people of the nation – his people now. He was calm and extraordinarily eloquent. He spoke of the Queen's close relationship with the Church of England, 'in which my own faith is so deeply rooted'. And he ended by thanking the millions of people who grieved for his mother and then proving that he believes in an afterlife: 'as you begin your last great journey to join my dear late Papa . . . May flights of angels sing thee to thy rest' – a quote from the final scene from Shakespeare's *Hamlet*, a character that Charles himself briefly played in 2016 as a four-hundredth birthday tribute to the Bard.

In part of his first Christmas address as King, in December 2022, Charles repeated his late mother's Christian ethos in an emotional tribute from the Chapel of St George at Windsor Castle: 'My mother's belief was an essential part of her faith in God, but also her faith in people and it is one which I share with my whole heart.'

*

Great Britain is up there with the best in the world at staging and executing ceremonial events, but there are always slip-ups, however small. The secret is not allowing them to show. The whole coronation spectacle was dazzling, from the Kings Procession from Buckingham Palace to the Abbey, with the horses glittering and sometimes getting over-excited in the rain, to the music both ancient and modern soaring through the rafters of the ancient Abbey. The ceremony itself was a moment for the country to unify in 'patriotism and pride'.

There was, however, a slight glitch, when the King's Procession reached Westminster Abbey ahead of schedule. An already irritated-looking King Charles was not pleased to be kept waiting and had to sit in the coach outside the Great West Door, canopied from the rain, for a full five minutes. The problem was that he had left Buckingham Palace two minutes early and the procession had travelled two minutes faster than scheduled as the horses had gone quicker than expected, yet the Prince and Princess of Wales and their children had left two minutes later than they should have done as their car had been forced to wait in Parliament Square until the mounted escort in front had moved. They entered the Abbey behind the King and Queen's procession and had to slip in front while Prince George of Wales, who was one of the Pages of Honour holding the King's weighty Robe of State, manoeuvred himself into position.

Queen Camilla's Lady in Attendance, the Marchioness of Lansdowne, also got held up and had to sprint along the wet pavement in her long dress to get to the Abbey ahead of the exhausted looking 74-year-old King and 75-year-old Queen. The night before, King Charles had held a reception for the visiting royalty and heads of state from all over the world, tagged onto a week that had been filled with other official engagements.

His mother had done it, with more receptions, banquets and engagements than anyone would have been able to imagine at the start of her seventy-year reign, but she was only twenty-seven when she was crowned and, thanks to her youth and beauty, never looked anything like as tired as she felt on that cold, rainy day in 1953. Fortunately, King Charles has inherited the extraordinary energy of his grandmother, who outlived the century she was born in. She, too, had faith in God, which helped her through the bad times as well as the good.

King Charles took his coronation vows very seriously. He remained focused on exactly what he had to do and felt his mother guiding him through each moment. He knows the future is in the hands of his son, the Prince of Wales, but he intends to make use of every moment he can to prepare the way for William and Catherine to keep the royal family relevant in the modern world.

His faith will help him.

13

HEIRS AND SPARES

Charles was never a spare; he was always the heir and treated as such. He was addressed and referred to as 'Your Royal Highness' from the moment he was born – a privilege also afforded to his mother, who began her life in considerable grandeur at the Mayfair home of her maternal grandparents, the Earl and Countess of Strathmore. Such was the snobbery of the day, the little Princess was spoken of as the first legitimate baby born to the commoner wife of a King's son in three centuries.

Princess Elizabeth was neither spare nor heir: she was third in line to the throne. She never said much about the prospect of becoming a future Queen except in a few very well-documented remarks first recorded in the book *The Little Princesses*, written by her governess Marion Crawford. But she certainly did not suffer because of her sudden elevation after her father became King. The family moved to Buckingham Palace and, according to Princess Margaret, the upheaval had its benefits. In an interview for BBC

Radio's *Desert Island Discs* in 1981, she confirmed that far from hating the place, 'Buckingham Palace was a very cosy house.' The two Princesses lived in the nursery apartments, which Margaret described as being 'high up' and looking over the Victoria Memorial in front of the palace 'so one could see the Changing of the Guard every day and that sort of thing.'

The nursery quarters became a place of sanctuary and security for successive generations of royal children. As we know, this was especially so for Prince Charles when he came back from boarding school and his mother was too busy to see him straight away – he always first made his way to the nursery.

Far from being lonely, royal children are always surrounded by people. The nursery staff become their friends, as do the children of the royal household. There is, however, always a difference depending on their heredi-tary pecking order. Princess Margaret resented being cast in the role of younger sister, though at no time did she ever indicate that she would like their positions to have been reversed. 'My sister and I were very close, although she's nearly five years older than me,' she explained. 'We never did lessons together, we always did lessons separ-ately, but then of course we had quite a lot of children who came to the [Girl] Guides for instance. We had a choir we used to sing in and there were the pantomimes and dancing class. One was brought up to be able to talk to anybody.'

What royal children weren't brought up to do was to

deal with their personal problems. Instead of learning how to cope with emotional situations, they were able to retreat behind the protection granted by their position. When Prince Andrew first met actress Koo Stark, for instance, he terminated his relationship with his previous girlfriend, Christina Parker, the following day. Overwhelmed by Koo but unwilling to come clean with Christina, he simply instructed the Buckingham Palace switchboard to stop putting her calls through and never spoke to her again – exactly as his great-uncle, the Duke of Windsor, had done when he ended his liaison with socialite Freda Dudley Ward.

However efficient that way may be when dealing with dispensable emotional wreckage, it was no method for dealing with the difficulties of married life – it is noteworthy that the marriages of Princess Margaret and Princess Anne ended in divorce, that the Duke and Duchess of York separated after only five and a half years and that the union between the Prince and Princess of Wales became marooned in incompatibility and hatred.

In Prince Harry's memoir *Spare*, his ghostwriter J. R. Moehringer paints a graphic picture of Harry's feelings about being second in line to the throne:

This was shorthand often used by Pa and Mummy and Grandpa and even Granny. The Heir and Spare. I was the shadow, the support, the Plan B. I was brought into the world in case something happened to Willy. I was summoned to provide back-up, distraction, diversion and, if necessary, a spare part. Kidney, perhaps. Blood transfusion. Speck of bone marrow.

That is completely untrue, of course, but it was how Harry chose to see it and allow it to dominate his life to the extent that he would eventually make a career out of it. He chooses to be the victim and wreak vengeance on the slights he thought he had suffered; on his family, on the press and through the courts. Before he married Meghan, Harry had a healthy dislike of the press, as he explained to me a few years ago when he was due to meet a group of correspondents at Kensington Palace. But he didn't become obsessed enough for it to dominate everything he did. Charles was always telling him not to read the papers or look online or at social media, but clearly to no avail.

As the spare, Harry was allowed greater licence than his elder brother. He would play the fool and get away with childish antics such as standing behind visitors and pulling funny faces behind their backs to make William laugh when he had to meet them. He showed an early talent for mimicry that took scant account of the importance of the person he was imitating. Both Charles and Diana were amused rather than annoyed by his antics, and even the Queen, so critical of William in his infancy, regarded Harry with grand-motherly tolerance.

Later events would suggest that more early discipline might have been helpful, but Harry wasn't going to be the one to complain when he was allowed to get away with his transgressions. He knew where he stood in the royal pecking order: at the age of nine he turned to his brother and declared, 'You're going to be King; it doesn't matter what I do.'

William, on the other hand, was increasingly weighed down by his situation. He became withdrawn and his head drooped in public. The sight of a camera made him uncomfortable. The matter-of-fact Harry was happy to get on with his life, taking the rough with the smooth without worrying too much about the consequences. William was different. As his introspection became more pronounced, he was more receptive to what his mother had to say. As is the way with children, the Princes were establishing their own individual relationships with their parents, and while Harry found he had more in common with his father, William was becoming closer to Diana.

There was no marked favouritism involved. Charles and Diana were careful to dispense their affection to their sons equally and their sons responded in kind. When it came to activities, interest and empathy divided the family into two camps. Harry became fascinated with guns and all things military. He pestered his father into taking him to Salisbury Plain to review the Gurkhas stationed there. They travelled by helicopter, both of them wearing combat fatigues. Harry was delighted and declared he wanted to be a soldier when he grew up. William, meanwhile, was quite content to spend the afternoons home from school curled up on the sofa in Diana's Highgrove sitting room. Explaining her sons' different characters, Diana once told me, 'William is very sensitive and Harry is very lively.' She added that 'William wants me to be there for him.' She was wrong about certain traits of Harry's, however, as when he married Meghan and left his homeland for America, instead of being happy with his increasingly luxurious lifestyle, his wife and his children, he became hell-bent on alerting the world to what he considered were the failings within the monarchy. The 'joker' Harry appeared to be a thing of the past and he revealed he had inherited some of his father's more unattractive characteristics.

When Prince Charles's press secretary Mark Bolland left his employ, he was given his own column in the now defunct *News of the World*, and in 2004, Bolland revealed some of the Prince's bizarre views. 'His biggest flaw is his self-pitying approach to life,' Bolland wrote. Charles used to express himself in memos, which according to Bolland 'all merged into one stream of bitter rage.' Bolland continued:

But it's principally his fault – something which he is (to use one of his overused-terms of abuse) genetically incapable of accepting. Rather like the Duke of Windsor, everything that goes wrong is someone else's fault. And he's developed an extraordinarily arrogant and petulant view of 'his vision' on almost any matter that is raised.

It is almost as though Charles embraces anything unconventional – and yet deep down, he is as conventional as it is possible to be. Charles is a contradiction in many ways. The organic loving gardener who lets his plants run wild is at odds with the man that insists on having a fleet of gas-guzzling limousines and sports cars.

Much of Harry's ire has been directed at his elder brother William, the heir, and their relationship has always been fraught with rivalry – so much so that Harry developed a complex about being second best. Diana called him 'her little baby' and he did not want to share her with William. Diana's friend and alternative healer Simone Simmons was called in to give him healing as he had been suffering from terrible headaches and struggled with dyslexia. Diana was concerned everyone was going to think he was 'thick' as he didn't have any thirst for knowledge and was not interested in sitting down with a book. He always felt the need to compete in everything, especially with his brother. His relationship with the Queen was very much characterised by Harry being the joker, and when he had something serious to say to her, he had very little idea of how to go about it, like his father before him.

Years later, when he was about to get married, Harry went to see the Queen to ask permission to keep his beard on his wedding day. The accepted rule is no beards when wearing military dress uniform. The Queen reluctantly agreed, as it seemed so important to her grandson. When William discovered this, he was furious: annoyed that Harry had gone to the Queen, annoyed she had given him her clearance and annoyed at what he saw as Harry's one-upmanship. William had not been allowed to keep his beard and had not been able to wear the military outfit of his choice at his wedding. He was the heir and he had to do everything by the book. Harry explains in *Spare* that William always felt the Queen indulged Harry in his misbehaviour, while he was expected to maintain high standards. This argument became so heated that at one point William actually ordered Harry to shave, 'as the Heir speaking to the Spare'.

As an adult, the closeness Harry had with his father as a child changed but they maintained an affectionate if distant relationship – at least, that was how Harry explained it to his ghostwriter.

Pa and I mostly coexisted. He had trouble communicating, trouble listening, trouble being intimate face-to-face. On occasion, after a long multi-course dinner, I'd walk upstairs and find a letter on my pillow. The letter would say how proud he was of me for something I'd done or accomplished. I'd smile, place it under my pillow, but also wonder why he hadn't said this moments ago, while seated directly across from me.

For many years Charles had a strained relationship with his mother. He claimed she never tried to understand him and he received more affection from his nannies than he ever did from her. And when his official biography by Jonathan Dimbleby was published, and then serialised by the *Sunday Times*, it coincided with the Queen and Prince Philip's historic visit to Russia. The Queen was furious that the serialisation of the controversial book had removed any interest in the visit from the press. The book detailed Charles's parental woes, including a lack of affection and understanding from both his parents. With Harry, it was the other way around. He had a good relationship with his father until he moved to America, 'unlocked his inner self' and started using his position as the spare to make a noise. He had discovered a way of making himself the centre of attention and that was by dissing his family, about whom he felt increasingly bitter. His row with his brother was one thing – this is not unusual with siblings, when one has all the responsibility and the other is free to have more fun. But the anger aimed at the monarchy, the British people, his father and stepmother, was totally unnecessary. His anger eventually destroyed his credibility in other areas of his life, and his grandmother the late Queen found herself in an impossible position. However much she loved Harry – and she did – she couldn't condone the way he was speaking about the institution of the monarchy that she had spent seventy years preserving.

Charles was embarrassed that he was unable to stop Harry upsetting the Queen by attacking what was, in essence, his and William's inheritance. Harry became so swept up with his role as spare that he even compared himself to his aunt Margo; he hardly knew her, but it struck him – as he says in his autobiography – that they should have been friends.

Lady Elizabeth Anson, who was a cousin and intimate friend of the Queen, and used to speak on the telephone to her on a daily basis, agreed that Harry's attitude had upset his grandmother. Lady Elizabeth explained that the monarch had originally been pleased that her grandson had at last found a woman to love who appeared to be able to return his intense passions. The Queen had liked Meghan on their first meeting over tea at Buckingham Palace, had high hopes for what she and Harry might be able to do, especially for the youth of the Commonwealth, and continued to champion her despite Prince Philip's warnings. He told Lilibet it was uncanny how much she reminded him of the Duchess of Windsor and duly decided to nickname her DOW.

Neither Charles nor Prince Philip was present when, in the middle of a windswept Norfolk field, Harry asked his grandmother for permission to marry Meghan. The royal family had just enjoyed a day's shooting and the Queen was picking up dead birds after the final drive with her Labradors. There were no security officers around her, so Harry realised this was his one chance to get his grandmother on her own.

He explained that however much he loved his paternal grandmother he still felt anxious in her presence which made him clear his throat nervously before starting to speak to her, telling her that he loved Meghan very much and that he'd been informed he needed to ask for permission before he could propose.

It was odd that Harry did not realise he had to ask the Queen's permission to marry. It was also odd that he had not told his father or brother first, and true to form the Queen gave one of her typically cryptic replies:

'Well, then, I suppose I have to say yes,' she said.

Harry was floored. He just didn't get it and wondered what his grandmother meant. He decided she must have been trying to be funny and he had simply missed the point. He must have been nervous as, despite his lack of conventional intellect, he is sharp and quick-witted. He finally worked out that the monarch was saying yes.

The Queen never voiced her true opinion except to her very closest confidantes, such as Lady Elizabeth Anson, or Liza as she was known to her friends. She told me that the Queen had made only one remark about Meghan and Harry's wedding and that was that Meghan's Givenchy wedding gown was 'too white'.

Those two words embraced everything she felt about the dramas in the run-up to the marriage and the Disneyesque spectacle of the day itself. Meghan had been married before and there she was, complete with the old-fashioned bridal symbol of purity: the veil. The Queen was also not comfortable with the Prince of Wales standing in for Meghan's father, Thomas Markle, and was similarly concerned about 96-year-old Prince Philip walking down the aisle without a stick, having had a hip replacement only five weeks beforehand. Like everyone else, she was startled by the impassioned spoutings of the American Archbishop Michael Curry, who spoke for over fourteen minutes. Both the Queen and Prince Philip hate long sermons and were desperate for him to finish, as was the rest of the congregation, many of whom were stifling their laughter. Curry himself, who admitted he did not know the couple beforehand, said the Queen 'was most gracious' and added he felt the presence of the slaves from whom he was descended in the chapel, which he felt to be a 'sign of hope'.

According to Lady Elizabeth, the Queen was dismayed by Harry's high-handed attitude both before and after the wedding, and their relationship was 'quite badly damaged by it all'. It was even more damaged when Harry decided to give up being a working royal and leave the country. 'I don't think the Queen ever truly understood Harry's decision to leave,' Lady Elizabeth told royal biographer Katie Nicholl. 'Turning one's back on duty is completely alien to the Queen and she has been very hurt by it all.'

Everyone hoped Harry would find happiness and on his wedding day it seemed within his reach. But less than three years later, having relocated to California and given a punitive interview to Oprah Winfrey in which he said his father was 'trapped' and the royal family were racist, Harry could not stop telling the world how many mental health issues he had. When he spoke on the *Armchair Expert* podcast, he said Meghan had identified his need for therapy shortly after they began dating in 2016. He insisted his pain was due to the fact his father had also experienced pain from bad parenting, which was then passed on to him as if genetically:

I started to piece it all together and go, 'OK, so this is where he went to school, this is what happened. I know this bit about his life, I also know it's connected to his parents, so that means he is treating me in the way he

was treated. How can I change that for my own kids?'
And well, here I am, I have now moved my whole family
to the US. That wasn't my plan, but sometimes you have
got to make decisions and put your family first and your
mental health first.

The Queen could have been the one who needed to put
her mental health first, but instead she did what she always
did – compartmentalised things. There was no point in
worrying about Harry as he was not going to take notice
of anyone except Meghan. William had had his problems,
too, but they had mostly resolved themselves with the
support and strength of his wife. The Queen had always
thought Charles and Diana's children were extremely
unruly little boys, which they were, but she had established
a relationship with William when he was still at school and
it stood him in good stead. Although he could not exactly
confide in his granny, they understood each other enough
to build a rapport. The Queen also enjoyed William's ability
to make Prince Philip laugh, and when they went duck
flighting together he could always get him out of his cantan-
kerous moods. Philip would come home cheerful and, if
not exactly full of bonhomie, was at least no longer grumpy,
for which the Queen was always grateful.

The Queen felt her son had pulled himself together and
done well with both William and Harry since the separation
and divorce from their mother all those years ago. After
the breakdown of the marriage, Charles had never had
much of a chance to have a meaningful relationship with

the boys, as Diana manipulated their time as one of her marital weapons. Whenever Charles wanted to have them with him for the weekend, Diana thought of an excuse to keep them with her, usually at the last minute. The Queen was well aware of this and worried about the damage the Princess was inflicting on her sons, especially William. No one worried much about Harry at the time as he was a happy, confident boy, completely at ease with himself.

William had plenty of problems. But he gradually began to understand the strength of the monarchy and how eventually it would be his turn to take the reins, however much he might not want to. He realised, too, that the luxury of having the independence to make his own choices did not mean discarding what had gone before. Continuity is fundamental to the royal family's role, which Diana never really appreciated but William certainly does, especially now his father is King.

William was at Buckingham Palace to see the outpouring of national pride that marked the Queen's Platinum Jubilee, and he witnessed first-hand the emotion that attended her passing. She had pulled the monarchy through the disaster of Diana's death and set him an example to follow. Since the days when he used to cross the bridge from Eton College to have tea with the Queen at Windsor Castle, William had been learning what it would take to fulfil his future role. He walked with his father and siblings behind his grandmother's coffin as it was borne on a gun carriage pulled by the King's Troop Royal Horse Artillery to Westminster Hall, where it would lie in state. It was the Queen's turn to take her place in the annals of the past. For William, it was another step on the steady march into the future.

Princess Anne was technically a spare until the birth of Prince Andrew, in February 1960, but while she was second in line for almost nine and a half years, she made sure she was first in everything else. She was hugely competitive with Charles when they were young and he never stood a chance against his wilful sister, even though she was two years younger. Everything he had, she wanted, and according to Anne they fought 'like cats and dogs'. When she was really worked up, she would throw things at Charles and lie on the floor kicking with sheer temper until she got what her heart desired. Charles was surprisingly gentle with his boisterous sister, and for all their squabbles they got along reasonably well. But if Anne was more than her brother's equal in the battlefield of the nursery, it was Charles who commanded the greatest attention. He was born to be King and that fact was subtly drummed into him and his sister from earliest memory.

By Anne's own account she 'always accepted the role of being second in everything from quite an early age. You adopt that position as part of your experience. You start off life as very much a tail-end Charlie, at the back of the line.' And however much she might have protested, it was there that she was destined to remain. She would, however, be grateful for this in years to come. She developed a healthy view of her position in the royal hierarchy, which allowed her to develop her own interests in her own way without the pressures of a centre-stage role that so inhibited Charles and William.

She was not so self-effacing as a youngster. As her author-ised biographer Brian Hoey observes, Anne would 'push her way to the front whenever she and Charles were together. If he held back when they appeared in public, Anne would be the first out of the car or train, determined that no one would miss her.'

Anne has a slight memory of being 'furious' her brother was going to their mother's coronation and she was not, but she also recalls being taken out onto the balcony after the ceremony and being told to wave 'to the people'. It was a public lesson in the demands that came with being a princess. There was no escape from being royal and, as she would later say, 'the idea of opting out was a non-starter.'

Instead, she opted out for her children when she refused titles for them, much to the Queen's disappointment, as Peter and Zara were her first grandchildren. Anne has always been close to her mother. They were friends and shared gossip and talked frequently on the telephone right to the end of the Queen's life. There was nothing the Queen could ask of the Princess that she wouldn't willingly do, and the same would apply if the Princess was asking a favour. 'It is more difficult to remember she is Queen than a mother,' Anne once said. 'After all, I've known her longer as a mother than as a queen. She has been Queen most of my life, but that's not how I think of her.'

On the last morning of the Queen's life, Anne was out

sailing on the Firth with her husband Tim – as she frequently did when she had some time to spare – during a break in engagements in Scotland. As soon as she received the emergency call on her ship radio, Anne and Tim headed for the shore and caught a flight from Inverness to Aberdeen. She arrived at Balmoral before the Prince of Wales and was able to meet him at the door of the castle. Anne took charge of proceedings as her brother struggled with his emotions, knowing not only that his mother was dying but that he was about to become King. As the Queen's only daughter, Anne assumed the role of unofficial hostess. She welcomed the rest of the family as they arrived later in the day – too late, as it turned out – and was there supporting everyone, especially her brother. Charles would have expected nothing less from the feisty sister who used to push him about, throw things at him and steal his toys. That night he returned to Birkhall with Camilla and William confident in the knowledge that Anne would take care of everything and everyone.

For twenty years, Prince Andrew enjoyed basking in the glow of being the spare behind his older brother Prince Charles and in front of his sister Princess Anne. Andrew could be charming but he was spoiled, pampered and, like his nephew Harry, nothing was ever his fault. He grew up with an inflated sense of entitlement and a sadly lacking sense of what was right and what was wrong. He thought he knew everything and was allowed to get away with it. He never referred to himself as the spare because he didn't feel spare. He felt important, as the head of what his mother called her 'second family', due to the decade age gap between him and Anne.

Colin Burgess, former equerry to the Queen Mother, knew Andrew and was remarkably accurate in his character analysis:

> The royal pecking order didn't sit comfortably with him. He saw himself as a military officer, as a war veteran who had done a lot for his country, including risking his life in combat, and as an ambassador for his nation rather than an armchair royal who sits on the trappings of power without actually ever doing anything. So, to deny him the luxury of royalty seemed pretty petty in his eyes and tended to cloud his outlook on life. In all honesty he wasn't a particularly nice person. He also was unable to relax and gave the impression of never being off duty without doing anything. He gave the impression he was there for himself and himself only.

As a child, Andrew was adored by both his parents, his nanny Mabel Anderson and the Buckingham Palace staff. He was spoiled, of course, then when he failed to reach all his family's expectations as an adult, his father berated him for being pointless. Philip was proud of his son's naval career but once Andrew came back from the Falklands, he never fulfilled his early potential. When he was the UK's Special Representative for International Trade and Investment, a role he took up in 2001, Andrew gained the reputation of tailoring his visits to include trips to luxury golf courses and fraternising with 'dodgy' Arab businessmen. The government realised this was doing serious damage to the British royal family and Britain's political, diplomatic and commercial interests. Around the same time, he was criticised for his association with Jeffrey Epstein, the US financier who was jailed in 2008 for the sexual abuse of underage girls. In July 2011, the Duke was forced to resign from his role. He had survived ten years as UK special envoy.

Andrew never got over losing his wife, Sarah Ferguson, or 'Fergie', when they divorced in 1996, but by remaining close to her and showing her loyalty when she most needed it, he invited her back into his life and into his home. She in turn stood by him and has done so throughout their many ordeals. It is hard for Fergie to see her former husband as the broken man he is today. He has lost his mother and the vital support she gave him. He genuinely loved the Queen and when she became frail and unwell would spend hours at Windsor Castle in her sitting room, watching TV with her and making her laugh just for the pleasure of her company. But she knew – and he finally realised – he will never be able to have any kind of military or royal status unless he finds a way to clear himself of the Epstein scandal and convince people he is innocent of any wrongdoing.

Unlike the Duke of York, William and Catherine's only daughter Princess Charlotte has kept her place as second in line, as in 2013 the Succession to the Crown Act replaced male-preference primogeniture with absolute primogeniture. This meant that Prince Louis, born in April 2018, remains third in line, though Princess Charlotte will only ever become Queen if Prince George predeceases her without having any living children. Prince William has never revealed if and when he told Prince George about his destiny, but I suspect, like his father before him, he will just accept it as fact.

The Queen always took a close interest in her grandchildren's welfare and would fuss around the nursery, moving chairs and rearranging toys when they came to stay. What did not amuse her so much was when William and Harry were older and naughtier. On one occasion they climbed onto the grand piano at Sandringham and Harry knocked a vase of flowers onto the floor where naturally it broke. Nanny was summoned to organise the clearance of the mess, but the Queen got to hear about it and was not pleased.

It may have been holiday time, but this was still a court bound by rules and conventions that had changed little since Victorian times. One of the first things William's nanny Barbara Barnes had been required to teach William and his brother was to bow to the Queen and the Queen Mother. This mark of royal respect to two anointed queens was rigorously enforced, as one of the long-serving members of the royal staff recalled: 'When they came to visit, the boys would wait by the door. When they entered, the boys bowed and then kissed them on the cheek and gave them a hug. It sounds a bit strange but it was not uncomfortable, it was so natural the boys didn't think anything of it.'

Nothing changes but everything changes. At the age of nine months, Prince George accompanied his parents to New Zealand and Australia, taking nanny Maria Teresa Turrion Borrallo with them. Back in 1983, William – also aged nine months – accompanied his parents and nanny Barbara Barnes on the same tour, where he was exhibited crawling on a rug in the grounds of Government House in Auckland for a posse of photographers.

At the age of ten, Prince William was attending the prep school Ludgrove in Berkshire. At the time of writing, Prince George is the same age and currently at Lambrook, also in Berkshire, the difference being that Lambrook is co-educational and Prince George is a day pupil together with his younger sister and brother. Like William and Harry before them, George and his siblings have the beautiful manners so necessary for royal princes and princesses: politely shaking hands, writing thank-you notes, coming down in their dressing gowns to say goodnight to whichever guests their parents may be entertaining – even the President of the United States, as it was when Barack Obama came to Kensington Palace.

Prince George has had an easier childhood than both his grandfather the King and his father the Prince of Wales. At almost ten years old, Prince George was a Page of Honour at his grandfather's coronation. At the same age, Prince William was dealing with the trauma of his parents' marriage breakdown. The Queen had been badly shaken by the separation and her staff noticed she was more partial than usual to her pre-dinner Martini. Even at that late stage, she was hoping that her son and daughter-in-law might yet reconcile their differences and get back together, if only for the sake of the children. It was always the children the Queen worried about, as they were the future and she knew young William had been through a lot.

Nineteen years later, Prince William married Catherine Middleton, who turned out to be the embodiment of a princess without having a drop of royal blood. Her very ordinariness made her perfect, and the Queen was pleased that the troubled childhood William had experienced was turned around with the support of the strong woman Catherine turned out to be. The power of the monarchy may have been whittled away but it remains central to the British constitution, and it will be up to William and his father to keep it there. King Charles, as the Queen knew, was the right person to keep the monarchy on track and, with the support of his wife Camilla, prepare it for William as she and Prince Philip had prepared it for him.

14

CONCLUSION

'The heart of a mother is a deep abyss at the bottom of which you always find forgiveness,' wrote the French novelist and playwright Honoré de Balzac. Those poetic words could have been crafted to express the seventy-four-year relationship between the late Queen and her firstborn son, King Charles.

Princess Elizabeth longed for a baby and, when Charles was born within a year of her marriage, it seemed reasonable to suppose that although his grandfather King George VI was exhausted by the war, he would continue to reign for many years.

The young Princess's hopes for her firstborn son to be raised 'normally' were dashed when the King died suddenly in February 1952, when Charles was just three years old. As a result, the people who were to be the most influential in his early life were two working-class nannies, Helen Lightbody and Mabel Anderson, rather than his mother. But, as with so many aristocratic children of the post-war era, Charles shared his mother's generation's manners and behaviours, which placed more importance on formality and self-control than affection and expression.

Nanny Mabel Anderson had the greatest hand in shaping Charles's character. She was gentle, organised and worked by a strict routine. She did the crossword in the *Daily Telegraph* every day at 11 a.m. while having her cup of coffee and listening to the radio. She provided both stability and security, and wherever they were in the world, her royal charges knew exactly what was happening in the Buckingham Palace nursery. It was unchanging and the same in the '60s, '70s and '80s as it had been in the '50s, and Charles carried this routine into his life.

According to behavioural specialists, Charles's conduct was partly fashioned by the formality of life in Buckingham Palace and the constant presence of the adults and their high expectations of him. This led him to become solitary and approach friendships with his peers with great caution. He was required to be tidy and neatly turned-out at all times, and his over-concern with appearance and things being just right has persisted all his life.

His mother understood nothing of all this, as the importance of early childhood was not on the agenda then and, even if she had known, there was little she could have done. Despite Charles's one-time criticism of his lack of parental affection, the Queen loved him deeply. He was her successor, her firstborn, and she was a lot warmer with him than she ever was with the young Anne.

The Queen was slightly mystified by the adult Charles,

as was everyone else, including Prince Philip, who felt that Charles's idealistic outlook was an unhealthy trait for a future King. He addressed his concerns to Charles in a series of letters signed 'Papa', many of which would carry some sort of reprimand in very much the same way as he later tried to help Diana, by writing her encouraging missives with a little sting in the tail but signed 'Pa'. Philip avoided face-to-face dressing-downs and preferred the letter or memo approach, as did Charles. The Queen was quite the opposite and let people know in person when she was displeased, telling them so and putting it to the back of her mind, though she never forgot. If anyone in her family did or said anything really stupid, however, she was more likely to express her displeasure through her private secretary Sir Edward Young, as in the case of the Duke of York and his disastrous *Newsnight* interview for the BBC in November 2019. Supported by the Lord Chamberlain Earl William Peel and Sir Edward Young, Charles, who was in New Zealand at the time, enlisted the help of his son, the Duke of Cambridge, in making his dissatisfaction known to Andrew.

Like his mother, Charles is sensitive to the plight of others, but like his grandfather George VI, he is intolerant of those who fail to offer him what he considers to be proper respect. Former footman Mark Simpson recalls one such moment back in the '70s:

I have heard him when I have been laying up dinner and he has been in his study next door screaming like crazy on the phone. Everybody would quake. He would clear his desk in one swipe. You could hear him sometimes in his bedroom. You couldn't hear what it was about but it was a huge, high-pitched scream. It comes from his grandfather. It is quite scary to witness. But afterwards he would be back to normal and be very polite and say thank you every six minutes. The rest of the time he was terribly gentle.

The Queen seldom, if ever, lost her temper and instead when things were going wrong tried to see the funny side of the situation. On one occasion many years ago, she was driving around the Sandringham estate in her Land Rover when it broke down. She had no detective with her and no phone, so she walked to a nearby farmhouse and asked if she could use their telephone. She then realised she couldn't remember the number of Sandringham House so she called Directory Enquiries and they wouldn't give it to her as it was listed as ex-directory! The Queen loved this story and enjoyed telling it at dinner parties, much to the amusement of her guests.

When Lady Diana Spencer moved into Buckingham Palace after her engagement to Prince Charles in 1981, the Queen made every effort to try to find time to spend with her, but because of her full royal schedule it had to be by appointment. The Queen's page would ring through and inform the footman looking after Diana what the Queen was doing that day and if she had any spare time to see Lady Diana. If, for instance, the Queen was free for supper, her page would ask politely, 'Would you join her?' Diana would immediately find an excuse, saying to her footman, 'I can't possibly have dinner with Brenda'. (Diana loved the way satirical magazine *Private Eye* parodied the royal family and called the Queen 'Brenda' and Prince Philip 'Keith'). Diana was nervous of the Queen as she didn't have anything in common with her at all and their conversation was always stilted. If Diana had tried to bond with her in those early days, she could have told the Queen her fears about Camilla. The Queen would then have been alert to the situation, and if she felt Charles was behaving badly, she would have called him down and told him off. As it happened, she only confided her worries to the Queen when it was far too late.

The Queen's stern look, inherited from her grandmother Queen Mary, belies the wonderful sense of humour we got to see more and more as she got older. The Queen could be extremely funny, in a slightly mocking way. She was also a first-class mimic, particularly of politicians, but never to anyone's face. She could only laugh or state her opinions in private, and some of them were pretty forceful. She also liked hearing a bit of gossip, so her immediate staff saved all the chit-chat for her about what was going on in every corner of her various homes. She saw everything but turned a blind eye to small misdemeanours and disasters. She was the same with her friends. At one Windsor Castle house party, the Countess of Sutherland became distraught when she walked downstairs to find she had an identical outfit to the one the Queen was wearing. The Queen looked at her, and for a fleeting moment the Countess wanted to sink through the floor, but she need not have worried. Pulling one of her hangdog expressions, the Queen turned around, saying, 'And guess who is going to have to change!' It was, of course, the Queen, who, being the perfect hostess, went upstairs and asked her dresser to select another frock. It is a story she enjoyed telling all her life – with certain embellishments.

In the final months of her life, the Queen had delighted audiences at the televised Platinum Party at the Palace after starting the festivities with a pre-recorded appearance with the fictional character Paddington Bear, in which they appeared to be enjoying tea together at Buckingham Palace. The sketch was filmed at Windsor Castle, with the Queen spending around half a day filming for the two-and-a-half-minute segment. It was a surprise even to some of her children, grandchildren and great-grandchildren.

The BBC and the Palace refused to spoil the 'magic' by explaining how the Queen was able to talk with the fictional bear without anyone being there, but it turned out that Paddington – voiced by Ben Whishaw, who had played Q in the recent *James Bond* films – had been filmed using just a mechanical head, before visual effects were added digitally.

Charles never enjoyed his mother taking part in things he considered undignified but even he had to admit it was a resounding success. He was, however, irritated when Angela Kelly, the Queen's dresser and later private assistant, persuaded Her Majesty to allow herself to be photographed looking like a model, with her hands in her pockets, something apparently she had always wanted to do. Kelly describes the photography session, which took place in the Throne Room of Buckingham Palace, in her book *The Other Side of the Coin*: 'The photographer Barry Jeffery kept his camera rolling as the Queen struck a series of poses, slipping her hands in and out of her pockets and placing them on her hips, mimicking the stances of a professional model.' One of the photographs was used for the front of Kelly's first book, *Dressing the Queen*, which included a couple of the images inside, too. It was enough to incur Charles's wrath – he felt it was thoroughly inappropriate, however good the photographs may have been. He was protective about his mother and thoroughly disliked what he considered was taking advantage of her good nature.

He could take advantage of it himself, though – and did. The lowest point in their mother–son relationship came in the early '90s, when Charles's spirits were depleted. His marriage was a sham, and everything else in his life appeared to him to be equally gloomy. Prince William was being petulant and seemed to the Queen's staff to have inherited the worst characteristics of both his parents. The Queen, whose dislike of divorce is well documented, thought that after the separation in 1992, such was the fuss and media coverage of the beleaguered couple, that perhaps a divorce might even be 'for the best'.

Charles in turn was blinkered and behaving, as far as everyone could make out, like the spoiled child he once was. He was determined to pursue things his way, believing he could do anything he wanted. It was around this time that Jonathan Dimbleby's authorised biography was published, with bitter claims from Charles that he was brought up by nursery staff, not his 'emotionally reserved' parents. This provoked an outpouring of criticism of the Queen's mothering abilities, forgetting that she had been preoccupied with affairs of state from the age of twenty-five and however much she might have longed to be with her children, was prevented from doing so.

The Queen was a master of the understatement delivered in her best deadpan voice as one of her closest friends, Lady Elizabeth Anson explained to me. 'Too white', referring to Meghan's wedding dress, meant it was not appropriate for a divorcee getting remarried in church to look quite so flamboyantly virginal. 'Too grand for us' was a remark she made to Lord Mountbatten as he was relaying the virtues of Marie-Christine's noble lineage before she married Prince Michael of Kent. 'Too in love' was her response to Prince Harry being under his future wife's spell. 'Too presidential' described the former Labour prime minister with whom she never gelled, Tony Blair.

King Charles may not quite have his late mother's acerbic wit; he is more of an orator, sprinkling his conversations with Shakespearean quotes (much as Boris Johnson tries to do with his Latin phrases), but Charles certainly has her devotion to duty. When he ascended the throne, he was dealing with difficulties from his son the Duke of Sussex and from his brother the Duke of York, but he quickly corralled his slimmed-down monarchy and got on with the job of being a figurehead that people could look up to and feel reassured by in turbulent times.

Charles is reassuring. When I sat with him at Highgrove in his Lloyd Loom wicker garden chairs, he made me laugh as we talked about him hanging by his feet from the ceiling to help the pain in his back. As he demonstrated a polo shot to illustrate where it hurt, his blazer, which had been on the back of his chair, fell to the ground. He just left it there and made no attempt to pick it up. *This is a man who has had valets and footmen all his life*, I thought, which of course he has. The Queen would never have done that – for all her position and grandeur, she was a simple woman at heart, a 'housewife *manqué'*, as Elizabeth Anson used to call her. She would have picked up her coat.

On a visit to the Prince's Trust charity ahead of Prince Charles's sixtieth birthday, the Queen spoke publicly of her pride in her son and what he had achieved. It was the first time anyone can remember such a warm public utterance in his favour: 'For Prince Philip and me there can be no greater pleasure or comfort than to know that into his care are safely entrusted the guiding principles of public service and duty to others.'

Mother and son had publicly reconciled. And when his 'darling mama' died, fourteen years later, he was able to embrace his role as her successor with his own special brand of warmth and humour, which has become characteristic of the new reign.

BIBLIOGRAPHY

Barry, Stephen, *Royal Secrets: The View from Downstairs* (Villard Books, 1985)

Barry, Stephen, *Royal Service: My Twelve Years as Valet to Prince Charles,* (Macmillan, 1983)

Bedell Smith, Sally, *Charles* (Michael Joseph, 2017)

Benson, Ross, *Charles: The Untold Story* (Victor Gollancz, 1993)

Bradford, Sarah, *Elizabeth* (Heinemann, 1996)

Bradford, Sarah, *George VI* (Weidenfeld & Nicolson, 1989)

Burgess, Major Colin, *Behind Palace Doors: My Years with the Queen Mother* (John Blake Publishing, 2006)

Buxton, Aubrey, *The King in His Country* (Longmans, Green & Co., 1955)

Crawford, Marion, *The Little Princesses* (Cassell & Co. Limited, 1950)

Dimbleby, Jonathan, *The Prince of Wales* (Sphere, 1998)

Ferguson, Ronald, *The Galloping Major: My Life in Singular Times* (Macmillan, 1994)

Friedman, Dennis, *Inheritance: A Psychological History of the Royal Family* (Sidgwick & Jackson, 1993)

Greig, Geordie, *Louis and the Prince: A Story of Politics, Intrigue and Royal Friendship* (Hodder & Stoughton, 1999)

Hardman, Robert, *Queen of our Times: The Life of Elizabeth II, 1926–2022* (Macmillan, 2022)

Hardman, Robert, *Queen of the World* (Century, 2018)

Hoey, Brian, *Anne: The Princess Royal* (Grafton Books, 1989)

Jebb, Miles (ed.), *The Diaries of Cynthia Gladwyn* (Constable, 1995)

Junor, Penny, *The Duchess: The Untold Story* (William Collins, 2017)

Junor, Penny, *Charles: Victim or Villain?* (HarperCollins, 1998)

Kelly, Angela, *The Other Side of the Coin* (HarperCollins, 2022)

Kelly, Angela, *Dressing the Queen: The Jubilee Wardrobe*, (The Royal Collection Trust, 2012)

Levin, Angela, *Camilla, Duchess of Cornwall: From Outcast to Future Queen Consort* (Simon & Schuster, 2022)

Litchfield, David, *Bailey and I: Bailey and Litchfield's Ritz Newspaper, Vol. 3* (First, 2023)

Lownie, Andrew, *The Mountbattens* (Blink Publishing, 2020)

Lumley, Joanna, *A Queen for All Seasons: A Celebration of Queen Elizabeth II on her Platinum Jubilee* (Hodder & Stoughton, 2021)

Mabell, Countess of Airlie, *Thatched with Gold* (Hutchinson, 1962)

Majesty magazine, various issues, 1985–2023 (Rex Publications)

BIBLIOGRAPHY

Menkes, Suzy, *Queen & Country* (HarperCollins, 1992)

Morrah, Dermot, *To Be a King* (Hutchinson of London, 1968)

Morton, Andrew, *Elizabeth & Margaret: The Intimate World of the Windsor Sisters* (Michael O'Mara, 2021)

Morton, Andrew, *Diana: Her True Story* (Michael O'Mara, 1987)

Murphy, Charles, *The Windsor Story* (Granada, 1979)

Nicholl, Katie, *The New Royals: Queen Elizabeth's Legacy and the Future of the Crown* (Hachette, 2022)

Parker, Eileen, *Step Aside for Royalty* (Bachman & Turner, 1982)

Peel, Sir John, *The Lives of the Fellows of the Royal College of Obstetricians and Gynaecologists 1929–1969* (William Heinemann, 1976)

Pimlott, Ben, *The Queen: Elizabeth II and the Monarchy* (HarperCollins, 2022)

Prince Harry, *Spare* (Bantam, 2023)

Seward, Ingrid, *Prince Philip Revealed: A Man of His Century, 1921–2021* (Simon & Schuster, 2021)

Seward, Ingrid, *My Husband and I: The Inside Story of the Royal Marriage* (Simon & Schuster, 2018)

Seward, Ingrid, *The Queen's Speech: An Intimate Portrait of the Queen in Her Own Words* (Simon & Schuster, 2016)

Seward, Ingrid, *The Last Great Edwardian Lady: The Life and Style of Queen Elizabeth the Queen Mother* (Century, 1999)

Seward, Ingrid, *Diana* (Weidenfeld & Nicolson, 1998)

Seward, Ingrid, *Royal Children of the Twentieth Century* (HarperCollins, 1993)

Seward, Ingrid and Unity Hall, *Royalty Revealed* (Sidgwick & Jackson, 1989)

Shawcross, William, The Queen Mother: The Official Biography (Alfred A. Knopf, 2009)

Strober, Deborah Hart and Gerald S. Strober, *Queen Elizabeth II: The Oral History* (September Publishing, 2021)

Townsend, Peter, *Time and Chance: An Autobiography* (Collins, 1978)

Turner, Graham, *Elizabeth: The Woman and the Queen* (Pan Macmillan, 2002)

Van Der Kiste, John, *George V's Children* (Alan Sutton Publishing, 1991)

Windsor, The Duchess of, *The Heart has its Reasons* (Michael Joseph, 1956)

Windsor, The Duke of, *A Family Album* (Cassell & Co., 1960)

Windsor, The Duke of, *A King's Story* (The Reprint Society, 1953)

Acknowledgements

A son's relationship with his mother is always interesting, especially in the royal family when so many formalities come in the way of motherhood – or they certainly did in the late forties when Prince Charles was born. I would like to thank the many people who have helped me through the journey of this book, which goes back to when I first started writing about the royal family and was introduced to the then Prince of Wales by his polo manager, Ronald Ferguson, at a cocktail party for the Guards Polo Club at the Berkeley Hotel.

Many of those who contributed are no longer here – in particular, my late husband, Ross Benson, who always entertained me with tales of Gordonstoun School where he was in the same class and house as the then Prince of Wales. The back copies of *Majesty* magazine have been invaluable in uncovering long-forgotten interviews I had conducted and provide a more reliable source than most things online today. I once spent an afternoon at Highgrove with the

Prince of Wales thanks to his then private secretary Commander Richard Aylard and have talked to many people who have worked with him, almost all of whom have fond memories of their generous boss.

I would like to thank my agent, Piers Blofeld at Sheil Land, for his wise observations and help; my publishers, Simon & Schuster UK; my editor Alison MacDonald, who has been endlessly patient and encouraging; along with Ian Marshall for his faith in my original idea. I would also like to thank Angela Levin whose excellent book on Queen Camilla was also published by Simon & Schuster UK and the authors of the many books I have used in research, in particular Jonathan Dimbleby, Robert Hardman, Katie Nicholl, Geordie Greig, Andrew Morton and the late David Litchfield, whose three volumes on the *Ritz* newspaper have jogged my memory for some interesting anecdotes and even more interesting times. I would also like to thank the many people who have over the years told me some delightful stories, many of which I have included in this book.

Finally, I would like to thank Nick Cowan for his encouragement and help with the structure of this book, his research and endless patience.

Ingrid Seward, London, 2024

INDEX

INDEX

INDEX

INDEX

INDEX